# WHO DIVORCES?

For every 3.7 marriages there is one divorce; and for every divorce, there are perhaps thousands of couples who remain together through sheer fear or shame of divorce.

But marriage doesn't succeed or fail in statistics. It is a human institution for human beings with human problems—and human solutions.

> Here, then, is a book to treasure. Simple, brief, compassionate and wise, it helps to bridge the gaps between loving people and people who wish to love, to enable them to find true joy in the sacrament of marriage.

# YOUR MARRIAGE— *DUEL or DUET?*

Louis H. Evans

FLEMING H. REVELL COMPANY
OLD TAPPAN, NEW JERSEY

The lines of T. S. Eliot's "Choruses From 'The Rock'" are from *Collected Poems* by T. S. Eliot, copyright, 1936, by Harcourt Brace & World, Inc. and reprinted with their permission.

The various excerpts from the writings of Dr. Paul Popenoe are gratefully acknowledged.

Scripture quotations in this book, except as otherwise noted in "Sources," are from the *Revised Standard Version of the Bible*, copyrighted 1946 and 1952, and are used by permission of the National Council of Churches of Christ in the U.S.A.

YOUR MARRIAGE—DUEL OR DUET?

A SPIRE BOOK
Published by Pyramid Publications for Fleming H. Revell Company

Spire edition published April, 1972
  Second printing February, 1973

Copyright © MCMLXII by Fleming H. Revell Company
All Rights Reserved

Library of Congress Card Number: 62-8411

Printed in the United States of America

SPIRE BOOKS are published by Fleming H. Revell Company
Old Tappan, New Jersey 07675, U.S.A.

## THIS BOOK IS DEDICATED

*to the homes and hearthsides of our four children and their partners, which have meant so much to us:*

MR. AND MRS. ROBERT S. DEATS
THE REVEREND AND MRS. LOUIS H. EVANS, JR.
THE REVEREND AND MRS. GARY DEMAREST
THE REVEREND AND MRS. WILLIAM O. EVANS

# Contents

| | | |
|---|---|---|
| INTRODUCTION BY DR. PAUL POPENOE | | 9 |
| I | Duel or Duet? | 13 |
| II | Your Marriage—Everybody's Business | 15 |
| III | The Sanctity of the Vow | 19 |
| IV | The Necessity of a Central Aim | 23 |
| V | Add Royalty to the Routine | 29 |
| VI | Responsibility | 36 |
| VII | Christian Disposition | 44 |
| VIII | Do Not Expect Too Much of Each Other | 51 |
| IX | In Honor Prefer One Another | 55 |
| X | The Regal Humility | 59 |
| XI | Finance—A Fury or a Fellowship? | 64 |
| XII | The Soul Needs Bread | 70 |
| XIII | Spiritualizing Sex | 73 |
| XIV | Adjusting Ourselves to Each Other | 78 |
| XV | Thankfulness and Thoughtfulness | 83 |
| XVI | Spiritual Oneness | 85 |
| XVII | The Head of the House | 87 |
| XVIII | You Mold Each Other | 91 |
| XIX | Forgiveness | 96 |
| XX | The Church and the Home | 102 |
| XXI | Keep Yourselves From Idols | 103 |
| XXII | The Home and the Home Town | 108 |
| XXIII | When a Couple Prays | 115 |
| XXIV | Your Shields of Brass | 122 |
| SOURCES | | 127 |

### IN APPRECIATION

My sincere appreciation is extended to Mrs. Julia M. C. Drake who during the writing of this book has been a most resourceful and helpful research secretary. Her tireless and efficient search for and arrangement of materials have been of inestimable help to me in the preparing of these messages.

# Introduction

No civilized country has as great a breakage of marriage as does the United States. In some circles "serial polygamy" has become established as an accepted pattern. Juvenile delinquency, virtually all of which stems from unsuccessful homes (with an excess among both the very poor and the very rich), is properly creating more and more alarm. Someone has calculated that, in the average divorce, twelve persons are directly affected; the rest of the community indirectly. As Louis Evans says, this is really "everybody's business."

The financial cost of all this marital disintegration is enormous, when both direct and indirect losses are reckoned. The cost in impairment of personality and in actual human misery is incalculable. Worst of all, failure in marriage perpetuates itself indefinitely into the future, for abundant evidence shows that marital happiness "runs in families." Men and women who are the products of happy homes are much more likely to produce such homes on their own account. Men and women who are the products of unhappy homes are much more likely to make a failure in their own marriages.

No one supposes that every marriage can be a good one. There are too many persons legally competent to marry but quite incompetent to succeed in marriage. Any realistic discussion must start by eliminating the pathological. No one can be expected, by any effort, to create a normal marriage when yoked to a partner who is to a severe degree mentally diseased, alcoholic, homosexual, or disabled in various other common ways. But the great breakup of marriages in the United States, involving some 400,000 couples—800,000 husbands and wives—each year, is not mainly based on such pathological cases. It is found among very ordinary people who started into marriage with high hopes and expectations, and ended in a few years in the divorce court. Why? That is one of the most important questions to which an answer must be found. That is the question to which Dr. Evans addresses himself.

Briefly, there is abundant evidence to prove that almost any two reasonably normal persons can make a success of marriage if (1) they know what to do, and (2) they do it. Even Dr. Kinsey, who approached the subject from a very different point of view from that of Dr. Evans, concluded unequivocally that the main factor in a successful marriage is the determination to succeed.

Don't people ordinarily go into marriage with a determination to succeed? I'm afraid the answer must often be No. Some go into marriage with the idea that it's merely an experiment; they'll see how it turns out and if they aren't satisfied they can quit any time they feel like it. Many more go into it with the idea that somewhere in the world there is a predestined Soul Mate to be found, and that when this Great Love appears (and it will be recognized intuitively), the rest of life will be an effortless ecstasy. If it turns out that some effort is required, it is clear that this was not the real Soul Mate after all; there was a mistake of identification and the only thing to do is to get out and try all over again, hoping for better luck next time.

Few people go into marriage consciously with such a crude picture of what is involved as I have here caricatured, but unconsciously they are not far from it. Consider for a moment the influence of all the "mass media": popular fiction, motion pictures, television, radio, popular songs—even the magazine advertisements and the billboards—all give an impression of Love as a mysterious visitation which comes unexpectedly and may go as unexpectedly as it came, quite beyond human control. Much of the failure of marriage is based on the adolescent type of fantasy, well named Romantic Infantilism by the psychologists.

There is plenty of evidence to prove that persons who have had good courses on marriage and the family, in high school or college, and who have acquired some rational and adult ideas in place of those I have just described, are more likely to succeed in marriage. There is now plenty of evidence that, even after a marriage is in great difficulty, it may be reorganized and put back on the track by marriage counseling which will root out these harmful notions and show husbands and wives what to do and what not to do.

But there is great need for much wider circulation of these facts. Men and women need to be told how to proceed; then they need to be inspired to go ahead and apply what they know.

The great merit of this little book by Louis Evans is that it gives the reader precisely these two kinds of help.

PAUL POPENOE

*The American Institute of*
 *Family Relations,*
*Los Angeles, California*

# I
# Duel or Duet?

MARRIAGE IS A fascinating subject. Most of the readers of this book are either married or they could be at any moment. That is immediately compelling!

Marriage is of vital interest to God. God is love. All the world loves a lover; so does God. This, after all, is His idea, and His pattern for life. The Scripture says: "There be three things which are too wonderful for me, yea, four which I know not: The way of an eagle in the air; the way of a serpent upon a rock; the way of a ship in the midst of the sea; and the way of a man with a maid" (Proverbs 30:18-19). The last is the most thrilling and bewildering of all the mysteries.

The difficulty with marriage is that it may either be a duet or a duel. God willed it should be a duet—that the two should be very closely one: "So God created man in his own image, in the image of God he created him; male and female he created them" (Genesis 1:27). "Therefore a man leaves his father and his mother and cleaves to his wife, and they become one flesh" (Genesis 2:24). "So they are no longer two but one. What therefore God has joined together, let no man put asunder" (Matthew 19:6).

This oneness is not easily or automatically come upon. In one of Paul Popenoe's helpful pamphlets, the story is told of a woman who came to a counselor and said, "I suppose I'll have to grin and bear it [she was doing anything but grinning]; after all, marriage is bound to be like that. It starts off with a high pitch of happiness, and then it slumps and drags along. It then becomes a dull monotony. [Only to dull folks. Mate dullness to dullness and you get dullness.] We will have to endure each other, or hate each other; that is life."

Another young couple said, "If, during our stormy matrimonial voyage, we do come to occasional patches of calm sea, we cannot enjoy them; we are so seasick from the other experiences."

Someone writes that in the colonial days there was but one divorce in about 500 marriages. By the year 1812 there was one divorce in every 110 marriages. The latest figures show one divorce to every 3.7 marriages. Some sociologist—in a rather melancholy mood, I fear—prophesied that if this curve keeps up, in seven years there might be one divorce to every 1.52 marriages. I think this is rather a pessimistic outlook, but the essence of the truth is here. Too many marriages have turned out to be duels.

But there is the other side of it. We may be optimistic about marriage in many ways. One other woman said to her counselor: "Marriage is wonderful. Tell young people that marriage can get better and better. Life begins at forty. Our honeymoon was an idyll, yet as I look back, any one of our trips was ten times better than our honeymoon. It is natural for marriages to improve year by year." Marriage can be a duet, and though marriage is a gamble, it is the type of gambling that every clergyman would recommend. But we must remember this, that Cupid does not run a romantic "ski-lift" which carries us to the top of the mountain of romance and then allows us to "slalom" down with ease, across the steep slope that lies ahead. A marriage is a climb, and sometimes a steep climb. But, holding on to the hand of God, the sights are wonderful up there—if we learn how to stay on the heights.

# II

# Your Marriage— Everybody's Business

A YOUNG COUPLE came to my office in Hollywood some years ago and said, "Well, Dr. Evans, we think our marriage might go on the rocks, but after all, that is definitely *our* business."

I said, "Don't talk like that! Your marriage is everybody's business!" And it is.

Marriage is a *nation's* business. When a pier juts out into the ocean, it is utterly at the mercy of the individual pilings on which it stands. Strike out a piling from beneath it and the whole structure suffers a shock and the pier is weakened. Every nation juts out into the social sea, resting upon the pilings of its individual homes. Every time a home is destroyed, the whole nation suffers a severe thundershock. No nation can stand for long with one quarter of its pilings gone, or damaged.

It may be that Edward Gibbon's 1788 analysis of the *Decline and Fall of the Roman Empire* is no longer passé, but strikingly contemporary. We see evident parallels between that society and ours: the rapid increase in divorce, undermining the dignity and sanctity of the home; the increase in taxes (and in the case of the Romans, the expenditure for free bread and circuses for the benefit of the populace); the present mad craze for pleasure; the building of gigantic armaments to the neglect of the real enemy within—the decadence of the people; the decay of religion, with faith fading into mere form, losing touch with life and becoming impotent to warn and guide the people.

Your marriage is very much the nation's business. The decay of the American home as the national unit is one of the most perilous characteristics of our age.

Marriage is definitely the *child's* business. The child is like a seismograph. It registers every domestic earthquake and every marital shock. Sociologists tell us that they very seldom see a case of disintegration in the personality of a child but that can be traced back to either a broken or an unhappy home. The home can make a child fall in love with love or else can scar it with antisocial instincts and fixations. Too many children are scarred today in the battles that are waging between parents. Somehow they always stand in the way of the blows and can seldom be shielded from them. Marriage is very much a child's business.

Marriage is very much *God's* business. God finds Himself in the difficult situation of endeavoring to explain His infinite character to our finite minds. When a boy builds a house of blocks, he can only build as large a house as he has blocks with which to build. When he runs out of blocks he stops building. If you and I build up the inherent, infinite character and nature of God, we must do it by means of blocks of our experience, syllogisms, and parallelisms that we understand. When we run out of blocks we stop defining God in a very definite way. Most of these blocks by which God explains Himself are domestic blocks.

"As a father pities his children, so the Lord pities those who fear him" (Psalm 103:13). Here, through a father's pity and understanding, God is able to explain Himself to the child. But if a father is not pitying, nor understanding, then God loses that means of explanation.

"As one whom his mother comforts, so I will comfort you . . ." (Isaiah 66:13). If a mother is not comforting, then that block of experience is gone.

". . . there is a friend who sticks closer than a brother" (Proverbs 18:24). But if a brother does not stand by, then that syllogism, too, is gone.

"Husbands, love your wives, as Christ loved the church and gave himself up for her" (Ephesians 5:25). This is a very objectionable instruction to some people because their marriage has been one that tragically failed to function, nor does it portray this deep, high, close relationship that Christ has with His Church. Thus, when a home is destroyed, God loses one of the greatest theological seminaries in the world, one of His chief ways of explaining Himself. Marriage is very much God's business.

It is difficult to build the home today for various reasons. They used to reënforce the old cathedrals with "flying buttresses." The cathedral was thus held together by outside pressure. Now most churches are built with cantilever construction, with inner ties hidden away in the masonry. The home of yesterday was kept together largely by outside pressure, in much the same way "flying buttresses" were used. You simply could not afford to be divorced. If you were, you were often isolated and people drew their skirts aside; you were passed by on the city street. Not so, today. Only a relatively small number of persons frown upon divorce today, or consider this sort of domestic breakage a sincere tragedy.

A century ago it was economically dangerous for a woman to be separated from her husband, for as yet industry and business were not ready to accept her as a wage-earner. Thus she might be facing financial impoverishment and even starvation. Now, the average woman can go into the market place and often earn as much as her young husband, newly launched on his professional or business career. The woman who stays married today stays married because she wishes to do so, not because she must.

The outside pressures that once held the home together have changed their nature, and social pressures of today are more likely to cause a crash in the home than they are to preserve it. This has made the situation much more difficult than in former years.

There is one factor in marriage which makes us both pessimistic and optimistic—that is the fact that the home is made up of individuals. Individuals being fickle, marriage often proves to be the same. But individuals being changeable gives us the hope that the home and marriage picture may be changed. Someone has said, "People don't dislike marriage; after marriage they dislike each other." Of course, you can never change marriage without changing people. Marriage is made up of human equations. It is not primarily an institution. It is two people, human beings, combining together to do something. Whenever human selfishness barges in, difficulties arise. The trouble with defining marriage as merely an "institution" lies in the fact that in this word you have three "I's" and only one "U." And the minute the you gives way to the I and selfishness pervades, we have the decay and destruction of the institution of marriage.

Let us consider now some of the factors that will make marriage a duet instead of a duel. Let us pose the problem from this simple syllogism: marriage is a triangle—one side, the husband; one side, the wife; and the base, the extrovert base, is God and unselfish religion. Let us consider together now some of the segments that make up that base of marriage, without which any home can collapse.

# III

# The Sanctity of the Vow

WHILE MOST RELIGIONS attach a certain sanctity to marriage, Christianity does so in a special sense. Christ said: ". . . For this reason a man shall leave his father and mother and be joined to his wife, and the two shall become one. So they are no longer two but one. What therefore God has joined together, let no man put asunder" (Matthew 19:5,6,7). Here is tenacious continuity, even finality, making up one of the characteristics of the marriage vow.

You will notice first of all that these twain are *one*. Of this Paul says in Ephesians: "This is a great mystery, and I take it to mean Christ and the church; however, let each one of you love his wife as himself, and let the wife see that she respects her husband" (Ephesians 5:32,33). I doubt if our human minds have ever quite grasped the mystery of the *oneness* that God wills there should be in marriage. This is a mystical union which God takes very seriously.

There is nothing like it amid all the human relationships of life.

God never said that a father and his son are an entity. They are two individuals and they go their separate ways. God never declared that mother and daughter are one. They are not. They are two vital, separate entities and they each find their own paths of duty and destiny. But God did say that husband and wife are one: ". . . they are no longer two, but one." Like the Siamese twins, they may be separated, but unless it is done with extreme care, and under the right conditions, something dies. Marriage is not an easy slipknot to be untied and severed with one tug of a quarrel, an intellectual or dispositional tussle. It has a continuity that is astounding when we analyze it in the mind of God. So close is this union in His mind that He gives it as the symbol of the eternal relationship between Christ and His Church. It has been used of God as He woos humanity, in His endless love.

"What therefore God has joined together, let no man put asunder" (Matthew 19:6). And man, on his own, cannot sever what God does not sever. Is there a sense in which our names are joined as truly on the books of God as they are on the record of the County Recorder's office? A North Dakota judge once said to a young couple, "According to the laws of the State of North Dakota, I must declare you free from the bonds of marriage, but may I remind you that probably on the books of the Almighty God you are still husband and wife." That is straight talk.

A judge in New York City some years ago gave this charge to the jury in a divorce case, and I think it is worthy of note:

I charge you, gentlemen, that so far as any religious

or sacramental, or church bond existing between these people, we have nothing whatever to do with it. If you decide for divorce in this case, remember you only cut the knot tied by the state's law, but you absolutely do not touch the religious or sacramental bond which states that persons are married, "until death do them part." When we are through with this case, that obligation is left untouched. We do nothing whatever to it. People are just as much bound by it after we get through with them as they were before. We do not sever it—we do not break it, and that is something that it seems to me is very often misunderstood.

Here was a member of the judiciary allowing his own judgments to bow before the authority of the judgments of God. In the mind of Christians the grounds of secular divorce ought to agree with the grounds of spiritual divorce. We have not time here to go into the various ramifications, discussions and theories regarding the grounds for divorce in the light of Scriptures. We may, however, say this: they are not as numerous as most people would think. There is a divine and holy tenacity here that is saluted by God.

*Religio* is a word from which we have derived our word "religion." It means, in part, "I am bound, I have an obligation." That obligation is to God, on the perpendicular. This sort of divine obligation immediately adds to the longevity of marriage.

Someone has stated that in Pilgrim Plymouth Colony, composed of some 70,000 persons, over a period of seventeen years, there were only six divorces. Why this constancy of vow in marriage? It was not that the Pilgrim Fathers were necessarily easy to live with under every condition. Someone has said, "Our Pilgrim Fathers Sunday mornings fell on their knees in prayer, on Monday mornings they fell on the aborigines in massacre." But there was a sense of "oughtness" that seized them here; it was almost as dependable as the law of "must." We have an obligation toward God, to our children, to our church, to our society, and to ourselves. Most people can "make it go" if they will, and these, our forefathers, willed it.

Here, in one interpretation of the marriage vow (secular and not spiritual) we have the possible short-lived contract expressed in these words by an unknown author:

> My love is like the poppy spread,
> You pluck the flower, the life is dead;
> Or like the snow falls on the river,
> A moment white, then melts forever.
> Or like the borealis race
> That flits 'ere you can point the place,
> Sign here, my dear, five years!

On the other hand, that marriage vow which is taken in sanctity in the Presence of God may lead to a story such as Robert Burns describes:

> O my Luve's like a red, red rose,
> That's newly sprung in June:
> O my Luve's like the melodie
> That's sweetly play'd in tune.
>
> As fair art thou, my bonnie lass,
> So deep in luve am I;
> And I will luve thee still, my dear,
> Till a' the seas gang dry.
>
> Till a' the seas gang dry, my dear,
> And the rocks melt wi' the sun;
> And I will luve thee still my dear,
> While the sands o' life shall run.

## IV
## The Necessity of a Central Aim

I WAS MAKING my way on a train between Los Angeles and Chicago and a young man in the Air Force, about to graduate from one of our middlewestern state universities, fell into conversation with me: "I'd like to talk with you for a few minutes. I am engaged to be married. I'm in love."

To this I said, "That has been perfectly evident. I have been watching you for two days and you have been glowing like a Bunsen burner!" (You can usually tell a young man in love, although you can't tell him much.) But this man was earnest and you could see he was making an honest inquiry.

He went on to say, "I am engaged to be married to the daughter of one of the leading bankers of our Ohio town. If I do what she wants me to do, namely, go into partnership with her father on graduation, I will make probably twice the salary I would make if I do what I wish to do."

I said, "What do you wish to do?"

He said, "I would very much like to become a professor in my alma mater and train men. But what I want to know is this—would she be happy on half-rations, on half salary?"

To this I found it necessary to reply, "I cannot answer that because I do not know her. What is she living for?"

To this he replied in some confusion, "Well, of course, I never asked her that, you know."

To this I countered, "Well, what are *you* living for?"

"I honestly have no idea, sir; I know I am going to make a living, but I have no definite idea of what I am living for."

Then I said: "Why are you two getting married?"

To this he replied with a winning, enthusiastic smile, "Well, you see, sir, we love each other!"

"Well," I replied, "if that's all there is to it, you can get so tired of that after a while you could spit at it!"

He said, "What do you mean?"

We talked. I tried to explain how the thing that keeps the solar system together is the fact that there is a great sun at its center. Put anything less than that there, and the solar universe flies to pieces. A home is like a solar universe—it revolves around a central sun, a great spiritual purpose. Put anything less than that there and the home can fly to pieces. I never saw a home go to pieces that did not lack a central sun. I have never seen a home triumphantly stay together in the deepest and highest ways that had not found that sun of a great unselfish purpose.

I said to him, "Now, look what you are doing. You are going to put your wife at the center and say, 'You are my sunshine, my golden sunshine'; but she is not. You will be making a little goddess out of your wife and some day you will discover that she has her weaknesses. Then what will become of your goddess? Your home will fly to pieces. Or, if a woman puts a man at the center of the home, as some have done, and says, 'My whole home revolves around my husband; it is built entirely around him!'—I cannot help but say within my heart, 'What a tragedy!' All men have feet of clay and when a woman discovers that, what becomes of the little mas-

# THE NECESSITY OF A CENTRAL AIM

culine god? Marriage is not two people living for each other; it is two people teaming up to live for God—the utterly dependable, Perfect Sun.

"We are made to *love* each other, but we are made to *worship* God. Unless this great central *design* is on center, unless we have a central spiritual sun, such as: 'Seek ye first the kingdom of God, and his righteousness . . .' (Matthew 6:33), we cannot expect longevity for our domestic system. On what are you two teaming up?"

Finally he replied, "Well, I'll go home and talk it out and we will find something around which to revolve."

To this I answered, "Find *Someone* around whom to revolve. Try the Son of God and His Kingdom."

All studies show fewer divorces in religious marriages than in secular marriages. When a home revolves around a central "design," a central spiritual "sun," it has a much greater chance of standing than it would have without God. God gave us the great design around which to revolve.

## LISTEN WORLD

You can't leave love to luck.
Love first came with leaping ecstasy.
But when this passes . . . as it always may . . .
Love, too, will go unless you make it stay.
For there come times when hearts
Are deaf and dumb, when nothing wakens,
Nothing yearns or burns . . . These times must come;
They are not accident, nor do they prove
Your choice of love was wrong.

They come with every lover,
Every loving bond . . . mother or father,
Sister, brother, mate. Always, at times,
Love seems as cold as hate. . . .

Cut off forever, by malignant fate.
But it's not so . . . Such chilling of the heart's
As much a part of life as thirst or hunger. . . .
It's the natural ebb of our affection's flow.
Such times must come for all who love,
And when they come you must know why,
And how to meet them or your love will die.

You can't leave love to luck,
You must at times build love.
Though lacking all delight,
As blind men weave a pattern in the night,
Counting each gentle gesture,
Spacing word and smile, groping through word and darkness
Of both heart and head, as blind men fumble
With their unseen thread.
Until at last from out the dull
Gray warp and woof of service, unto God and men,
There's the shine of that sweet wonder
Which you had thought had passed. . . .
And, once again, you feel God's beautiful design.

If two persons are to be "one," they must have discovered somewhere an "adhesive." They must have found something strong enough, warm enough, vital enough to have brought about this welding process: some alchemy that has enabled them to combine, some heat of purpose that has enabled them to fuse in mind and soul, some force greater than themselves to hold them together. If they have not discovered this, two individuals with two individual purposes will war against each other in a dynamic, pathetic duel.

One of three principles governs the modern marriage, and we shall have to make our choice of one of these.

Principle number one is husband and wife trying to *conquer* each other. This inevitably leads to a

## THE NECESSITY OF A CENTRAL AIM

duel. Once in a while you see a husband who is able to conquer his wife. He has the fallacious idea that marriage is an ownership rather than a partnership. If he does succeed in subordinating his wife completely, he becomes as obnoxious as an army sergeant and she becomes mousy and impersonal. This is always a tragedy.

Sometimes the wife attempts to subordinate her husband and succeeds in doing so. This type of bumptious and overbearing woman is immediately disgusting to society at large. Her husband becomes henpecked—a pathetic, shrinking soul and dominated personality. One day a very angry wife said to her henpecked husband, "Harry, are all men fools?" To this he meekly replied, "No, dear, some are still bachelors!"

> When you, my lordly love, hold forth
> On subjects ranged from south to north;
> From up to down, and east to west,
> You'll note how rarely I protest
> Your dictums. Sometimes this is due
> To the fact that I agree with you.
> Other times, with guile concealed
> I deem it strategy to yield
> On minor issues; so I may gain
> 'Vantage for a larger fray.
> But now and then I just prefer
> The peace that rules if I concur.

The second principle of home operation is husband and wife *worshiping* each other. This is equally dangerous in the other extreme, and inevitably leads to disappointment. We have already mentioned the possibility of a man and woman putting each other at the center of their home, endeavoring to deify and worship each other. One woman made this great mistake of worshiping her husband, and wrote these lines upon discovering his weaknesses:

> Because I believed God brought him to me
> And because I believed him gifted of God
> With honor, truth, and the love of the right,
> I believed in God and I worshiped God.
> But when I found he was just a thief of love,
> When I found he was full of treason and prejudices,
> All for money and worldly pride—
> The wreck of him was the wreck of God.
> I fainted amid the ruin of plaster and sticks,
> And sat in the stillness that followed
> The broken bust of God.

Our hearts belong to each other but our souls belong to God: "You shall love the Lord your God with all your heart, and with all your soul, and with all your mind" (Matthew 22:37). We love each other but we worship God.

The third system is this: *God* conquering the husband with His selfless spiritual purpose, *God* conquering the wife with His selfless spiritual purpose—and then they stop trying to conquer each other. Then they are one in the purpose that now conquers and controls *them*—the will of God. This immediately begins to transform the duel into a duet of one single increasing purpose for both. These are now alternate beats of the heart of the same great purpose. Thus the twain are in the deepest sense one—they have united in marriage to serve God.

# V

# Add Royalty to the Routine

MOST THINGS IN life tarnish. Sterling silver must be repolished; the lustre of chrome slips away; the first thrill from an expensive hat is soon lost; the job that once enthralled us takes on a dismal pallor.

This can be true in any profession. James Gordon Gilkey tells about a letter he received from a schoolteacher some time ago:

> I wonder if you could help me with one of my personal problems. I have been teaching for a number of years and long ago all the newness wore off my work. Like most teachers in the thirties I have now settled down to a regular and a painfully familiar routine. My difficulty is that I often find myself beset by an almost unconquerable restlessness and dissatisfaction. Some days it seems as if I wouldn't continue teaching another minute. When that mood passes it is followed by a mood of complete indifference toward my job. I lose all my interest in teaching. I realize that such feelings will be detrimental to the quality of my work, and I have tried repeatedly to conquer them. But in spite of all my efforts they keep coming. If you could tell me how to master these moods of restlessness, and maintain a steady interest in my school work, I should certainly appreciate it.

A sort of dullness that attaches itself to some duties is often found by those who deal with humanity. There is something in the human equation that takes a great deal out of us, that tests our sense of newness and freshness, and here there is every possibility of "going stale" in our contact with human hearts.

It can also happen in the church. Many a minister starts in his new parish with a sense of freshness and eagerness, but constant contact with the pale of mind, the frightened, the fearsome of heart, the visionless one, and the natural lethargy of the human heart, tends to strike down his new enthusiasm. A steady succession of difficulties and problems beat down that spirit that once was fresh within him. The town skeptics are upsetting, and the golf and country clubs have a tremendous pull upon the schedules of his people. For a while he may seem to be rescuing many of these from the secularism that touches their minds and their schedules as well, but when he finds himself losing these again to the world, to their primary secular interests, a certain restlessness gets hold of him. Then he must read a new sense of privilege and opportunity into his daily tasks.

This feeling will often attach itself to our domestic life. Married life starts off with a honeymoon, thrilling, compelling, and new. It makes little difference where it is celebrated—in a single room, in a spacious hotel, in a cottage by the sea, or in some forest primeval, chosen as this first rendezvous of a thrilling love. The shopping is fun, and the husband considers it a lark to wear the apron, and pick up the dishtowel. Work is fun and the sound of wedding bells is everywhere.

Possibly that same environment, after a while, has a much paler nature. The cry of a youngster can be very strident, the odors of cooking lose their tang, the noise of dishes and the clanging of the phone no longer are bell-like. Instead they have become merely boisterous and upsetting. A sudden conviction that housework amounts to nothing, or to very little, gets

## ADD ROYALTY TO THE ROUTINE 31

hold and the "great beyond" of a career, of a business world's attractions, of the warmth and fuss of the social whirl lay hold of the feminine mind. The domestic atmosphere can suddenly seem foggy and even choking; its once thrilling surroundings become rather confining, the kitchen seems like a dungeon in which one is hopelessly incarcerated, and before long a restlessness creeps in. Some of the dignity begins to fade amid the pressures of what seem to be common duties. Of course, the changes are in us and not in the things we are doing. The mind has a paint brush of attitude and with it colors everything—in somber hues, or with lavish thrilling colors.

It is necessary to find some recipe for keeping this eternal lift that must accompany the load, to maintain this royalty that must add itself to daily routine. When this metamorphosis of mind and the consequent change in our evaluation of what we are doing takes place, we must find something that will hold us to the job. One of these things, of course, is the necessity of continuing in our present obligations. Some people stay by their jobs because there is no honorable way of escape. Having trained themselves for a certain vocation, it is too late to change. It is very difficult, of course, to change horses in the middle of the stream. When once we have gained a type of technical and professional training for a certain avenue of service, it is very difficult to start down another avenue, stripped of the accouterment and equipment that we have taken to ourselves for the other sort of travel.

The minister is trained only to be a minister. The teacher is versed in pedagogy now, and the man of business knows the market better than he knows the other areas of life. It may seem that no swapping of responsibilities is possible, and it is futile sometimes to look for a happier situation. For this reason many people just sort of succumb, out of duty and necessity, to the unsatisfactory place into which they have maneuvered themselves.

This sense of "must" or at least a deep sense of "ought" attaches itself to the marriage vow. The Christian does not find himself or herself able to just "walk out on it" without the frown of God, to whom a much more binding vow than this has been made and in whose Presence has been said something like "Until death do us part."

Another facet of this problem presents itself to us here. There are difficulties in every profession, including that of marriage. Every profession has its disconcerting characteristics. There is an element of risk in any vocation a man can embrace: promising things do not always fulfill their promises; securities in the market have proved themselves to be insecure; industry does not come up to the prophecy we had made for it; the patients treated prove to be most thankless; and the shaping of the human mind and destiny in the field of education is so slow in progress that it makes us restless and strikes us down, at times, with discouragement.

It is not surprising, then, that in marriage and in the home there are some disappointments. God has not chosen that the married state be devoid of everything difficult, disappointing, and hard. Marriage, as well as any other career, is a testing ground for our courage and character, and a school of patience and long-suffering. These things must not so much bewilder us and frighten us—they must challenge and develop us. Marriage is a climb. It is a task. It is a challenge. It is a happy struggle. In this profession we are sharers of the experience of all the other callings in the matter of hardship and ease, laughter and tears, songs and sighs, victories and defeats.

Another of the things that must keep us steadily on this marital course is the fact that we are dealing with and influencing human lives, characters and personalities. There is no more important value in life to God than the human equation—what is happening to people. *And we are doing things to people constantly as we walk together.* When we share our courage with each other, we are sharing it with someone made in the *image of God*. The simple art of cookery (or the complicated cuisine) has to do with the nourishment and health of the body, which is, after all, the temple of God. The happiness we share with each other is reflected upon all those who see us face to face in any day's task and in every hour of moving about. The serene quietness or the agitated upheaval of the morning breakfast table is carried out into the workaday world and influences all with whom we come in contact. In the personal problem of getting along together we all are part of the collective problem of society, or we are a part of its happy solution. Every restless wave adds to the social tumult of the sea, and every patch of quietness in our souls adds to the tranquility of a world that is hungry for peace and poise. Our actions undoubtedly bring not only ourselves but the other nearer to God, or drive that person from Him.

The family altar has brought a certain guidance and quietness which we radiate throughout the day, or our godlessness and secularism is added to the riot and restlessness of our own and others' minds. No couple live to themselves alone. We are all bound up in an inescapable bundle, and we affect each other mightily. Like soft clay, each molds the other. And this home product that we have fashioned together acts in society as either a model or a menace to those who view it, day by day and hour by hour.

This holy purpose of service to God and to others survives surprisingly well in different kinds of environment when the drive is pure and sustained by God. It works well in a hovel, or in a large house; in a single room, or in a mansion. Whether it wears the garb of affluence and wealth, the homespun of poverty, or dwells in modest circumstances, it lives merrily and mightily.

Again, this inner drive to "Seek . . . first the kingdom of God and his righteousness . . ." ought to receive a double radiance when we are able to seek the Kingdom together. But even in times of separation, this lamp has to keep on glowing, and the fire must keep on burning. The size of the salary has little effect, nor do the bludgeonings or ease of the day altogether determine it. If this is something to which God has called us, and to which we have pledged ourselves, then no matter what the outward circumstance, the inner compulsion is there and we must go through with it. Or better yet: we are pleased to see it through.

A New York newspaper reported this personal story:

> I was living at Sandy Hook when I first met my husband. He took me to that Lighthouse as his bride. I enjoyed the life there, for the light was on land and we could have a garden and raise flowers. But one day the Government transferred us to the Light on Robin's Reef, surrounded totally by water. The day we came I said to him, "I can't stay here, the sight of water wherever I look makes me too lonesome." I refused to unpack my trunk and boxes, but somehow they seemed to get unpacked and I've been here ever since. It is almost forty years.
>
> One night my husband caught a bad cold while tend-

ing the light. It turned into pneumonia, and they took him to the Infirmary on Staten Island while I stayed there to watch the light in his place. A few nights later, as I was sitting there tending the lamp, I saw a boat coming. Something told me the news it was bringing and I expected to hear the words that came up out of the dark.

"We are sorry, but your husband is worse."

"You mean he's dead?" I answered, and they made no reply. We buried him on the mainland over there. Every morning when the sun comes up I stand at this porthole and look toward his grave. Sometimes the hills are brown, sometimes they are green, sometimes they are white with snow. But they always bring a message from him. Something I have heard him say more often than anything else; just three words—"Mind the light!"

Is not this the supreme challenge? Many are looking to our home, to our marriage for the light of guidance, the encouragement that all need. For this sea is a desperate one and filled with innumerable dangers and when we keep this light burning in our hearts, in our loyalties, in our homes, then others see it and trace their course by it, past the dangerous shoals, past the hidden rocks, through the storm and into the harbor of success and God's peace. A trust like that should be enough to make us keep the light burning, whether we live in the circumstances of Robin's Reef or amid the flowers of Staten Island.

Titus wrote a letter to Paul complaining of the miserable place to which Paul had sent him—the isle of Crete. It was called by many "an island of abomination surrounded by water." There was little potential leadership there, and little of anything else but sin. Titus had room enough for complaint. Paul, who had sent him there to serve in such untoward circumstances, wrote him back a letter and said, "For this cause sent I thee to Crete." In other words, your reasons for leaving, Titus, were my reasons for sending you there. There was nothing there; you were the one to bring it. They were much in need; you were the one to supply that need. It was so unpromising and you were to bring the promise.

And Titus stayed by. Today there is outside the Cathedral of St. Titus a garden filled with flowers. There they bloom with a serene beauty to commemorate the one who stood by when it would have been so easy to flee. There will always be those coming to the courtyards of our homes to see there the flowers of the graces that grow in the garden of self-sacrifice and of constancy. To make these contributions in hearts and life and action without complaining is one of the great virtues of life. We must do it without pitying ourselves, rendering this service happily, for "Laugh and the world laughs with you, weep and you weep alone." There are some people who can name their marriage as a self-sacrificing service; but when they record their experience it is like peeling an onion—inwardly they cry all the while. Is this the most attractive sort of behavior? Let us glory in the task that He has given us to do, and do it with laughter and with good-willed enthusiasm.

# VI
# Responsibility

EVERY MARRIAGE MUST be approached by both husband and wife from the standpoint of a royal responsibility. Without this, the marriage relationship may be a cheap and tawdry attempt of each to outmaneuver the other in receiving rather than giving; in placing self before the two.

Many of the free-love enterprises, inordinate experiments of living together, are based on no sense of obligation. Paul Popenoe says:

> Why do people want to enter into a free-love union, when they could just as well marry? The reasons alleged are nearly always incomplete, and usually not the real reasons at all. But back of them all is what I believe most unprejudiced persons will admit to be the real reasons; namely, the desire to avoid responsibility.

If the two do not like it they can call it off and experience no further obligation to God, to the state, to society, or to each other—at least so they think.

Polygamy has often been based upon an economic motive on the part of the husband; the more wives he has the more free work he has done. "The poor man is benefited by having as many wives as he can get, since they represent so much unpaid labor." This idea is still extant in some places. When I was in Africa I noted that some of the native men had as many as a half-dozen wives. This was profitable since each wife maintained a truck garden and grew vegetables and other commodities while the husband was the grand superintendent of the work—the more wives, the more income.

I was in conversation with an Arab guide in the African desert some years ago. He was the owner of a hundred camels, some sixty private soldiers, and quite a retinue of servants. During the course of one of the trips, he invited me to his harem. This invitation I waived, but the conversation that followed was interesting. He stated that he loved two of his wives more than he loved the others. I asked him if he let them know of their superior place in his heart, and to this he vehemently replied: "No, never tell a woman you love her. She no work for you any more!" This was the aim—so much unpaid service.

Of course, there are some women who might easily have the same economic motive for marriage. Paul Popenoe goes on to say:

> Women probably err quite as often as men, in their unwillingness to carry their share of the load. The merely decorative, parasitic wife is a conspicuous feature of city life in this as in previous generations. The woman who thinks her husband's only occupation and duty are to entertain and gratify her whims is a frequent client of the divorce court.

Many a wife judges her husband's success by the size of the wardrobe he can purchase for her and how large a bank account he can put at her disposal. One husband suggested that his wife do some of the housework, to which she countered, "What do you think I am, a horse?" He replied, "I was only asking."

God always insists upon an equal sense of responsibility on the part of both husband and wife concerning the hearthside and the marriage contract.

The wife must see in the building of the home a very regal calling. I do not think we have come to the place where wifehood has outlived God's vision of industry which describes her in Proverbs 31. Let us glance at some of the phrases that fit together to make a part of her domestic responsibility:

> A good wife who can find?
>    She is far more precious than jewels. . . .
> She does him good, and not harm,
>    all the days of her life.
> She seeks wool and flax,
>    and works with willing hands. . . .
> She rises while it is yet night

# RESPONSIBILITY

and provides food for her household
and tasks for her maidens.
She considers a field and buys it;
with the fruit of her hands she plants a vineyard.
She girds her loins with strength and makes her arms
strong. . . .
Her lamp does not go out at night.
She puts her hands to the distaff,
and her hands hold the spindle.
She opens her hand to the poor,
and reaches out her hands to the needy.
She is not afraid of snow for her household,
for all her household are clothed in scarlet.
She makes herself coverings;
her clothing is fine linen and purple. . . .
She looks well to the ways of her household,
and does not eat the bread of idleness. . . .
Give her of the fruit of her hands,
and let her works praise her in the gates.

Now the spirit here is contemporary, though we must change some of the phrases. For the words "wool" and "flax" we might substitute cotton and silk. "She gives tasks to her maidens" might give way to, "She teaches her daughters responsibility." Instead of "considering a field and buying it," she does influence much of the spending money in the home. Someone has humorously suggested that men spend 90 per cent of their income on the women and the women determine how the other 10 per cent should be spent.

Instead of her "planting a vineyard," there are some that love to keep the garden in season. The rising "while it is yet night" might have something to do with the generous midnight snack for the man she loves or waiting for the children to come in. "Opening her hand to the poor" would mean that she takes some part in community philanthropies. She too "looks well to the ways of her household and does not eat the bread of idleness." For this reason, "Her children rise up and call her blessed; her husband also, and he praises her: 'Many women have done excellently, but you surpass them all.' "

It seems reasonable that a woman should approach the career of running a household with the same earnestness with which she expects her husband to approach the running of his business. Each should *excel* in his and her own realm of endeavor. The woman, of course, is the queen of the household, inasmuch as she is both its hand and its heart. So many young American girls approach the marriage contract without any serious consideration as to their preparation for making a happy home.

In the matter of the culinary art, it is not wholly true that "the way to a man's heart is through his stomach," for then any restaurant waitress or cook in a commercial kitchen could have access to his affection. But the man may see in the fact that the woman desires to be efficient in this act a gesture both of her devotion and her resourcefulness.

The home is a man's haven, and naturally he likes to see it well kept and functioning efficiently. This task is a part of a wife's adequacy. The same royalty of routine ought to preside over the present-day sewing machine as presided over the Oriental "distaff" of yesterday. The skill of commanding an electric oven ought to carry with it the same sense of ministry as pertained to the baking of bread in Biblical days. The costumes of service change, but the inner aims of service remain ever the same.

The husband has a definite responsibility as well. Paul admonishes Timothy, the young pastor, to command the men of his congregation as follows: "If any one does not provide for his relatives, and especially for his own family, he has disowned the faith and is worse than an unbeliever" (I Timothy 5:8). This battle for bread, this adequate provision on the part of a husband, is a part of the performance necessary in his well-rounded Christian function. This is always conditioned, of course, by his ability to do so. There are many conditions under which a man, through no fault of his own, is quite unable to be a provider at all and, in other cases, unable to provide adequately. The demands of the Christian home today are beyond that which any previous century has known; only a considerable whittling down of the appetites and the desires of both husband and wife can bring adequate provision within the realm of some salaries. But this is a fundamental drive of the husband's heart—the passion for provision.

This purpose of the husband enters into the problem at the time of marriage. Should a young man who has not as yet completed his education enter into the matrimonial contract when he perceives the impossibility of supplying adequate bread for the household by his own effort? Is it right and is it wise for him to accept the wife's part in this battle for bread in which she becomes a partial provider for the needs of the household? This arrangement can be made happily and by mutual agreement, but it must be accompanied by almost perfect understanding. The monthly bills will always agitate the naturally proud husband if he himself cannot meet the pressures. But if this is by common understanding, in order to furnish more adequate academic preparation for the husband that he may better provide in the years that are to come, then this may be permissible—but it is often problematical.

This co-provision, of course, has been happily performed in many a home when it is based on adequate understanding. A young woman who runs a power sewing machine many hours a week in a factory tells the following story of her married life:

My husband, left an orphan, never had a chance to go to school and learn a trade. He is a teamster. He makes very little money but he loves me enough to trust me with all he earns. We have nothing that rich people have and we are boarding until we can furnish a little home for ourselves. My husband does not go to saloons or places of that sort and he seldom goes out for pleasure without me. Do you think it hurts me that he cannot give me fine clothes when every day he tells me I am the best thing God ever gave him? Every night he kisses my hands that have worked so hard all day. We have been married over a year and never a cross word. I did not know anyone could be so happy. Do you think I mind working to help a man like that? His love makes everything worth while.

This man did not have a university diploma, nor any of the benefits that come from adequate business training, even in the technologies. Yet he had that rare gift that enabled him to make his home a heaven and a haven. Here was a fellowship of provision, and a co-partnership in bringing in the family salary on a basis of utter appreciation and understanding.

In this matter of an early marriage during the time when the husband is still studying, and when his income is thereby curtailed, a couple should never eliminate the possibility of the arrival of a child. Many a young couple has been quite set back by the fact that the "unplanned baby" has made its arrival. She was going to work quite unencumbered by any parental obligation until such time as they "could afford it." But the "best laid schemes o' mice and men gang aft a-gley," as Burns said. A young couple ought never to marry unless they feel definitely that the coming of a child to their home would not be considered an intrusion but a blessing. An unwanted child has "two strikes against him." When he breathes his first breath, the unwelcome spirit in which he begins his little life is picked up unconsciously and carried through the early years. Whenever the coming of a baby "destroys the pattern," then parenthood starts off at a miserable pace.

Often the woman considers the possibility of blending a career with marriage. There are both possibilities and dangers here. There is always the peril of a woman in a profession having her own set of interests and not contributing to her husband's courage and drive in his battle for bread. If two come home at night equally exhausted by the pressures of earning and the problems of a profession, then their problems incline to be "two," and their personalities incline to be "two." It is very difficult to throw one's dynamic affection into two careers—those of a helpmate and a wage earner.

If ever a woman's career gets in the way of her marriage, then by all means she should drop her career, for the home is her first obligation to God and she accepted it at the altar. If she can carry this career load, however, and still keep her life and personality a fresh haven of courage and understanding, attending happily to the duties of the household, then it can be a proper possibility. But if she siphons off her energy, her drive, her poise, her personality, and her affection in the world of work, she can, if she does not take care, find her home bankrupt in the realm of the spiritual and emotional ministries, those that a wife alone can render. Making a living must never eliminate the primary function of making a life —making it rich, full, happy, adequate.

The royal responsibility of the home must always hold its own with the fascinations of the world outside for the woman. Many a woman in a dramatic career, intoxicated by the applause of the crowd, the thrill of the stage, the acclaim of the multitude, in comparison found a child's cry very insignificant, the praise of her husband in competition with the praise of the mob, and the home taking on a rather pale and insipid color against the colored lights on the ways of recognition and applause from a world outside. She may look down upon the worn overalls, the threadbare business suit, and rather colorless nature of her husband's task, and begin to bask selfishly, and sometimes superficially, in the attractions of the more colorful careers that sometimes beckon the feminine heart.

# VII
# Christian Disposition

LIFE IS MADE up not only of doing what we ought to do but in doing it happily. The Bible says of a wife: "She . . . worketh *willingly* with her hands" (Proverbs 31:13). This word "willingly" means with rejoicing, and with a sense of privilege. The home is the most important institution in the world. It was founded even before the church was founded, and in a deep sense can be a part of its foundation. True, it is not as eternal as the church, but it has a great deal to do with the spiritual tone of our life.

As men must find a definite dignity in their daily task of provision, which is one of their partnerships with God the Father, so the woman must find some dignity in her domestic routine. There are times

## CHRISTIAN DISPOSITION

when kitchen utensils must thrill her more than an afternoon out; when she must see the bigness of what some call a little place; when beads of perspiration become diamonds in a crown of faithfulness; when, lacking the time to attend symphonies, she can hear the music in a baby's cry. Making a home is of more value, even, than making a reputation.

I like these words by an unknown poet:

> Lord of all pots and pans and things, since I've not time to be
>   A saint by doing lovely things or watching late with Thee,
> Or dreaming in the dawn light or storming Heaven's gates
>   Make me a saint by getting meals and washing up the plates.
> Although I must have Martha's hands, I have a Mary mind
>   And when I black the boots and shoes Thy sandals, Lord, I find.
> I think of how they trod the earth, what time I scrub the floor
>   Accept this meditation Lord, I haven't time for more.
> Warm all the kitchen with Thy love, and light it with Thy peace
>   Forgive me all my worrying and make my grumbling cease.
> Thou who didst love to give men food, in room or by the sea
>   Accept this service that I do, I do it unto Thee.

God has always been as much interested in how we feel as in what we do. It makes a great deal of difference whether the inner streams of our dispositions run along serenely or if they are made up of dashing cataracts, unpredictable and fretful in their courses. Someone said of a couple, "They are simply not fit to be tied." When we are too often "fit to be tied," we are not "fit to be tied." The serene, steady, vital Christian disposition is a *sine qua non* of the Christian life.

Solomon said: "It is better to live in a corner of the housetop than in a house shared with a contentious woman" (Proverbs 21:9). He echoed this thought when he said, "A continual dripping on a rainy day and a contentious woman are alike" (Proverbs 27:15). These words might have been spoken when he glanced from his palace court that housed too many wives to the sight of a bachelor making his bed alone, but serenely, on the corner of a housetop.

It was an Oriental torture to bind a man and let water drip upon his head, not torrentially but lightly and insistently, until he became insane. An ungracious little system of nagging can cause a man to lose his mental balance—and fussy housewives can fill half the men's clubs in the world.

On the other hand, there is no adequate defense for a man who comes home from work at night, tired and spent though he may be, being like an ogre and acting like a sore boil, very sensitive to the touch, and ensconcing himself behind the evening paper, daring anyone to interrupt his quiet. The wife ought to know and be sure whether or not a man is coming home to act as a "softie" or a ruffian. There ought to be more consistency in masculine behavior and our dispositions ought to be more predictable.

The atmosphere of a home is of tremendous importance. It does make a difference. The spirit of melancholy on the part of either the husband or wife can drop down on the home like a dismal, foggy, dark day. There is a vigor that belongs to a cool, crisp morning. There is a laughter that is natural when spring is in the air and the sun is shining. It is depressing to live always in a dismal atmosphere.

A woman has a great deal to do with the atmosphere of a home. She determines largely its light or its shadow, its melancholy, or its merry vigor. When a man has been away and working all day, when he has been cheated, maligned, bested, driven, called a liar, or unreasonably treated; when he has met with small souls that tested the elasticity of his patience and arrives home to get still more of the same, he experiences a sort of twentieth-century crucifixion. It is more than too bad when a man has to be further mauled by unpleasant home pressures.

A young man asked a Dr. Edwards for the hand of his daughter in marriage. Dr. Edwards refused—quite a setback for a young suitor. He said, "Why can I not marry your daughter? I love her."

Dr. Edwards replied, "I think you do."

"I can support her."

He replied, "I suppose you can."

"Then why can't I marry her?"

To this Dr. Edwards answered, "My daughter has a miserable disposition—nobody could live with her and be happy."

To this the suitor replied with real gallantry, "But you know, Dr. Edwards, there is always the grace of God."

Dr. Edwards smiled and replied, "When you are as old as I am, young man, you will realize that the grace of God can live with some people that you can't live with!"

I suppose that is true, and yet I wonder if the grace of God lives with anyone who cannot live with other people. Paul said, "Any one who does not have the Spirit of Christ does not belong to him" (Romans 8:9).

Feminine duties, whether they are domestic or in the realm of a career, take a great deal out of a woman's disposition; and these inner resources must be replenished, on the other hand, by a thoughtful partner. There is no adequate spiritual excuse for two people acting as flint and steel and always producing a spark. Two hearts do not need to be opposite poles; a Christian disposition is something possible to us all. It is true that some persons have more problems to adjust to than others, but this is no excuse for failure in this regard.

Most of the problems of evil dispositions come from inherent selfishness. They all bud from the same stem. The grapes of dispositional weaknesses cluster about and are nourished by jealousy, self-pity, introverted petulance and an unlovely concern for one's self. Self-pity throws us back upon the old problem of tearing self from the throne and not putting God there. "Do you seek great things for yourself? Seek them not . . ." (Jeremiah 45:5). This is the lesson unlearned by many. We become immediately petulant about the lack of appreciation of ourselves, the fact that we are not the recipients of proper praise. Our own ideas are crossed, and the petulances immediately set up; the offended personality begins to pout.

A Christian disposition in a man is more welcome to a woman than a handsome check. The woman who is adorned with a lovely disposition is royally clad, in a man's conception. A woman may be a good housekeeper but a poor homemaker. Any man, when he comes home at night, would rather see a happy smile reflected in his wife's eyes than to see his own visage mirrored in the bottom of a well-scrubbed frying pan.

A meal may be well prepared, but if it is not par-

## CHRISTIAN DISPOSITION

taken of in an atmosphere of friendliness, the appetite is gone; no amount of seasoning makes an unfriendly meal any more than insipid.

Why is it that some of us are so difficult to live with? Why are some women so short-tempered, so mean in disposition? Many times it lies in the fact that we are simply God-hungry. A woman went to her physician and said, "Doctor, I think I am on the verge of another nervous breakdown. I am short-tempered, I am mean, I lack self-control. I am incurring the disfavor of my husband and I am losing my children; God knows I don't want that to happen! What is the matter with me?"

After thorough examination, he said, "Organically you are perfect. You are fighting hypertension. This is what I prescribe. Get up fifteen minutes earlier every morning. Take your Bible—if you do not have one, buy one—read it for five minutes, then sit quietly for five minutes and think of what you have read, and then for five minutes talk to God. If you have not learned to pray, you must learn immediately. That is my prescription and that is all."

The woman bristled angrily and said, "I did not come here for spiritual advice. I came to you for a physical diagnosis."

He replied, "That is my prescription. And it will cost you $50.00." He smiled as he said it for he knew her well. She went out of his office in high dudgeon. But this was her last straw, there was nothing else to try.

She rose fifteen minutes earlier the next morning, took the Bible down from the shelf and blew the dust off it. She read it for five minutes. Then she thought of what she had read for a period. Then she tried to talk to God. This was very difficult. The water was way down in the pump—from disuse—and she had to prime it considerably before it came to the surface. After a few attempts she began to have conversation with God. Over a period of about two weeks, her nerves began to iron out and her temper quieted. She went back to the doctor and said, "I feel well."

He said, "You are well."

She said, "What was the matter with me? What do you call that disease that brought me such irritation?"

The doctor smiled and said, "My dear lady, you were simply God-hungry, that is all."

Could that be your trouble? Are you God-hungry? Have you been trying to feed your soul with a spoon? The soul is not nourished that way. A hungry tigress will easily rise and rend you; but when she is well fed the danger is greatly abated.

One day, a young man irritatedly slammed a door in Abraham Lincoln's face. Recovering himself, he said, "I am sorry, Mr. Lincoln, I am just upset today."

Lincoln put a kindly hand on the man's shoulder and said, "Young man, why don't you stop fighting God on the inside?" What a student of human nature! Many times we fight God on the inside and turn to fight everyone on the outside. I have seen many a man sign an armistice with Christ in his heart, and live at peace with other people.

There are reasons for irritability and some of them are spiritual. Prayer, when properly exercised, can have a tremendously quieting effect upon our natures.

> Lord, what a change within us one short hour
> Spent in Thy presence will prevail to make!
> What heavy burdens from our bosoms take,
> What parched grounds refresh as with a shower!

We kneel, and all around us seems to lower;
We rise, and all, the distant and the near,
Stands forth in sunny outline brave and clear;
We kneel, how weak! we rise, how full of power!
Why, therefore, should we do ourselves this wrong,
Or others, that we are not always strong,
That we are ever overborne with care,
That we should ever weak or heartless be,
Anxious or troubled, when with us is prayer,
And joy and strength and courage are with Thee!

Jesus said, "Blessed [happy] are the peacemakers . . ." (Matthew 5:9). "Notice the word," says Dr. C. Milo Connick. "Jesus does not say 'How happy are the peace*thinkers,* the peace*hopers,* the peace*teachers,* or the peace*preachers!*" Their assets are frozen. Peace doesn't just happen. It is *made.* Jesus declares that it is the peace*makers* who are happy!" You and I have to work at this matter of peace. It has to be pieced together by many attributes of Christian character. It is a divine mosaic that is the result of bringing into our lives those facets that make for peace—love, longsuffering, meekness, self-control, humility.

# VIII
# Do Not Expect Too Much of Each Other

IT IS HARDLY fair to appraise each other apart from our inheritance. When you marry a man, you marry his grandparents, and certainly his parents. The characteristics he absorbs and regrets, the lacks he readily admits, inwardly or verbally, trouble him as much as they trouble you. Some of the early bestowals that others enjoyed might not have been his. When you see a lack of drive in him, perhaps it is because he was born in a home of little ambition. No matter what the surroundings were as to material appointments, his town might have lacked that ambition and forward-looking vision that characterizes some hamlets and cities.

This spiritual maturity at which you feel he should have arrived, at least by this late hour, found no incubation in his young heart since his family never laid them down to rest on devotion's sod. The family altar and family prayers were no part of the lessons his lips had early lisped at his mother's knee. The stubbornness there is in him was a part of the unyielding process that surrounded him because the minds he knew arrived too quickly at selfish conclusions, and never allowed the bias to be tampered with at the hands of others. He does not make another try for he thought from early childhood that one defeat was final.

Maybe when it comes to a great patriotic sense, his forbears did not come over in the *Mayflower*. Statistics show that while we have two parents, four grandparents, and so on, the numbers leap, until back six centuries ago, we each had two million ancestors, and they each made their own gift to us in some way. It is through this mesh of influence that a person must fight his way, but the encouraging thing is that with God all things are possible.

Nor can a man expect his wife to possess much poise, perhaps, since her mother screamed so thoughtlessly in the household and yelled her commands, a sign that she was losing her grip upon her children. The viselike set of standards that are hers and her unrelenting unwillingness to share your difference of mind could come from the fact that in her cradle she wore the strait-jacket of a sort of over-pressured rigidity of behavior, making it quite difficult for her to remove the constriction and even laugh out loud with a merry heart. She may have seen her mother humiliated and revolted against, or subjected to things that deprived her of her rightful place as a woman. Having inherited a set pattern of life, she may revolt against the subordination of a woman's personality to a husband who is bumptious, obnoxious and overbearing. Yesterday echoes within us down through the halls of our personalities, and yesterday is strangely combined in the today with which we live in another's heart and life.

But let us not be forced into hopelessness because of these inherited traits. Mary was raised in Nazareth, but she was better than her environment. There was a harlot in Jesus' lineage, but it did not discourage Him. There is a possibility of being ". . . a new creature . . ." (II Corinthians 5:17) in Him, and with a toss of the head we can say, ". . . forgetting what lies behind . . . I press on toward the goal for the prize of the upward call of God in Jesus Christ" (Philippians 3:13,14). Christianity was never a case of "whence we came," but always "whither we are going." We are not responsible for our yesterdays, inherited. But we are for our tomorrows, intended.

It will help us to know and to understand that each of us may have to rise to a new tomorrow, in spite of a tenacious and adhesive yesterday, a yesterday that hates to let us go, and would cling to us quite violently. We need the other's patient help to shrug it off, and to brush aside its delays and its discouragements. This is a time to restudy, too, what heritage we shall leave our children, to mind the barriers and shun the handicaps, and be rid of those tendencies which, if inherited, would be millstones about their necks. This is a time to vow that our own parental lives will be the better steppingstones to higher things and that we somehow shall have made easier their swift climb to God, with worthy characters and attractive natures.

We can change. The study of human nature has proved beyond a doubt that even mature men and women can learn to do about anything they want to do, and can become almost anything they want to become, with the aid of God. In this sense, the clay of our personality never really hardens. At times it may be moistened with the tears of our humility, or the wax softened by the heat of our desire to be what we ought to be and to be better than we have been. The old dogs can learn new tricks. "If any man be in Christ he is a new creature" (II Corinthians 5:17). We can put off the old man. Then old things can pass away and all things become new. God is still a good repairman in any age and in any day. All that remains is our change, if we desire it, in the hand of the great Sculptor, and our willingness to be His clay.

With a God of power, what we have been need never be as mighty as what we may become. There is no place where the soul can be as optimistic as in the home, when love demands of us the desire to achieve our better selves in God. Let us look at each other always, then, not in terms of what we are, but what we can be. The prodigal—whether he be prodigal in disposition, in mind, in life, in character—can always be sure that One awaits him at the Father's house, and that there is ready a ring for his finger, shoes for his feet; and a renewed relationship with both the Father and with his brother. This is our supreme comfort; this is our supreme confidence.

# IX

# In Honor Prefer One Another

IN MARRIAGE WE must remember that we must live "in honour preferring one another" (Romans 12:10, I Peter 3:7). We have not married to insure the happiness of ourselves alone, but equally, if not more, to seek the happiness and efficiency of the other. Love "seeketh not her own" (I Corinthians 13:5). Love seeks the glory of the other.

In any of the denials of life, the willingness to undergo inconvenience, the willingness to allow our selfish pride to be shoved aside, the willingness to bear the occasional slights to our dignity that sometimes come our way, are most important. There must always be the glorification of the task that the other is doing. Our lack of composure and self-control rises out of the fact that self has been frustrated, that self has not been recognized, and that self has had to be kept waiting.

Bruce Barton tells this story of Abraham Lincoln:

In the early months of the Civil War, when no one in Washington knew how soon Lee's troops might reach the city, Lincoln and a member of the Cabinet went to call on General McClellan. Official etiquette prescribes that the President shall not call upon a private citizen, but the times were too tense for etiquette. Lincoln wanted firsthand information and McClellan was the one man in Washington who could give it.

The General was not at home and for an hour the

two men waited in his parlor. Finally, they heard him at the door and supposed, of course, that he would speak to them immediately. But without a word he hurried upstairs. They waited again—ten minutes, twenty, thirty. Finally, Lincoln asked one of the servants to remind the General that his visitors were still waiting. Presently the servant returned and with obvious embarrassment reported that McClellan said he was too tired to see the President. As a matter of fact he had already undressed and gone to bed.

When the two men were outside the house, the Cabinet member exploded in anger. Would not Lincoln instantly oust McClellan from command? But the President laid his hand quietly on the other man's shoulder. "There," he said, "don't take it so hard. I'll hold McClellan's horse, if he will only bring us victories."

What held Lincoln in this trying situation? Why was he willing to accept this slight, this seeming insult to his own dignity? Why was he willing in humility to be "kept waiting"?

There was a great purpose in his heart to win the war and to free a race—that was Lincoln's passion. Lincoln's pride, Lincoln's position, Lincoln's dignity took second place to the great purpose of Lincoln's soul.

You and I will have to subordinate ourselves humbly to great purposes.

Surely the woman who is a wife and contributes to the home in order to bring her husband victory in his daily tasks, in his profession, in his calling, will be willing now and then to undergo the slights that challenge the pampering of her soul. Masculine pride will put up with an occasional indignity because there is a cherished goal that lies in the hearts of both of them. Self is the greatest enemy to all of life—its leaden density sinks ships, causes, people, marriages, empires, and homes!

"Jesus . . . did not count equality with God a thing to be grasped, but *emptied himself*, taking the form of a servant. . . . he . . . became obedient unto death, even death on a cross" (Philippians 2:6-8). He would willingly suffer all this humiliation, this dethronement from His position, this lashing of His pride, if only somehow He could bring about the salvation of the race, yours and mine.

Something bigger than self must grip us in the home. Otherwise, situations will become unbearable, and the home's humiliations too disheartening. Our unwillingness to "take up our crosses," to put up with the burden when it cuts across our own particular desires, our own particular prides, and our own particular wishes, is the main barrier we throw across the progress of the Kingdom of God; across the progress of God's ability to use marriage as an unselfish tool in His service.

Many times our lack of composure in life is simply an evidence of self-enthronement. It is our inner personality pouting; it is our ego grieved; it is our haughty head that someone fails to crown each day with some tiara of praise. It is a sign of our betrayal of the highest purpose, to be of service to others and to God. Thus we are rendered useless in so many ways.

The surgeon must have a quiet confidence—above all, he must be calm under pressure. Any undue ruffling of his calm denies him clarity of judgment. He passes this turmoil on to his patient who therefore loses confidence in him. If this goes on, the doctor needs the operation more than the patient. As Christ, though in a smaller way, we are all called to be physicians and healers of human hearts; but sometimes we are more the *patient in need* than we are the *physician of helpfulness*. We become the objects of sympathy and concern in the home; we who should be comforters are suddenly in need of comforting, and we who should be helpmeets become those who most need to be helped. It is very difficult for anyone to put up with these lapses of self-control and these tantrums of self-pity, and only most untiringly sympathetic hearts can continue to endure them and still love with that abandon that we expect of them, even when we fail so miserably.

Of course, on the other hand, there is always God's challenge to patience with the other, which is our continuing privilege in the marriage contract. At times we simply expect too much of other people. Some have backgrounds from which they are unable to escape. It is true that "it is too late to change our grandfathers." But some people still carry them around on their backs. Heredity is a tenacious cocklebur, difficult to remove from the clothing of our personality. We pick up still more of these "burs" in our daily contacts in the social walk. We meet people who are physically and nervously upset. We meet unreasonable persons, unfortunate persons. We are constantly the target of innuendos, falsehoods, and indiscretions. The average heart is not very successfully armored against these things and we must be patient. Some people have inherited fears; they suffer from frustration; they have the memory of many dreams that never came to fruition. Some people are just naturally nervous—inherent poise has never been nature's gift to them. They acquire it only after considerable struggle. Some people are not just naturally lovely—they have to acquire loveliness.

The great patience of Jesus lay in part in the fact that He ". . . knew what was in man" (John 2:25).

Knowing that their struggles, their temptations, and their inherited tendencies were human, he cultured Himself in kindness, in forbearance, and was not overvexed when they let Him down. It is a merciful thing that ". . . he knows our frame; he remembers that we are dust" (Psalm 103:14).

There is an artistry here of treating every man and woman as a "child of God." We look upon them and we love them, not always because of what they are but in terms of what they ought to be, and *what they can be as children of God*. Jesus was always loving His disciples for their potential, as well as for their performance. He called them the "light of the world," although many times they were dim. He called them "the salt of the earth," though many times they had lost their savor. And all the while He was looking ahead and seeing in men what they could be if He helped them—and if they permitted Him to help. This vision must never die out in the home.

# X

# The Regal Humility

OUR FIRST URGE, when criticized, is to defend ourselves and not to admit the need. A confession of sin is far more a sign of character than a cocky contention of our supremacy. In any argument in the home, our first tendency is often a furious defense of ourselves and our own position rather than a salute to the other's appraisal. We must win our point—and in doing so we often lose our man!

A woman conquered can be a woman lost, and a woman enthroned can also be a woman enshrined in the heart. Many times our great upheavals of mind and disposition in the face of criticism rise not out of the fact that we are confident that the other is wrong; but rather, from a consciousness, even unadmitted, that the other is right and that our weakness has finally been discovered. Instead of admitting it and proceeding to repair it, we deny it and its insidious roots go the deeper.

It is strange that the hardest censure for us to receive is that which comes from the lips of those who are dearest to us, and who oftentimes are the most qualified to appraise us. Perhaps this is because love hates to offend, and we are most conscious when we have offended, by failure, the one we love. This may be too pretty a picture of our offended pride; sometimes we are not forlorn because the other has been hurt, but rather because we ourselves have been hurt and our pride severely wounded. It will take a very clever analysis of ourselves to know just which of these two things is happening when criticism comes.

Here is where our devotional life will help. The Bible is a mirror in which we see ourselves—frankly and quite unchanged. There, in the morning devotion —or the evening Bible reading—we see the untouched negative just as the frank camera of God's word has photographed us, with every wrinkle, every freckle, every displaced tress, every flaw of the complexion. Having looked in a mirror and seen ourselves, it will not suffice for us, as James said, to be like a man who "observes himself and goes away and at once forgets what he was like" (James 1:24). This is a time for arresting ourselves in thought and procedure and making such changes as the Scripture has revealed to us are utterly necessary and immedi-

# THE REGAL HUMILITY 61

ate. The other in the home quietly sees without comment how the Scripture has described us, and what ought to be done.

But we accept this from God more easily than we accept it from our dearest ones and the treatment will take place only because God has prescribed it to us and because we ourselves have been willing to admit our need of it. To proceed with the therapeutic is sometimes humiliating, but always healing. Two are quite blind if they do not hold up occasionally the mirror of God's Word and peer at themselves quite fixedly. Having seen the vision of themselves thus revealed, they are doubly unwise if they do not rise and with God's help make the change. It is true the other might see us through a lover's eyes and thus be merciful, and pretend to touch up the negative with the brush of an inherent mercy and forbearance. But this has not changed us, though the other be blind with love or too kind to mention what was seen. This deeper therapeutic, this vital change, must come upon us because we have bid God to work it in us and to bring it about at whatever cost to us.

The most practical and thrilling therapeutic characteristic in any home is our willingness and desire to see ourselves as we are in the mirror of God, to desire to change, and in submitting ourselves to Him, allowing that change to take place. At this personal operation, God the Great Physician presides, but Humility is a scrub nurse that hands Him constantly the instruments of change. Without the assistance of Humility at His side, these instruments are quite out of reach of His skillful and magic hands.

The constant carping, nagging critic in the home, whether it be masculine or feminine, becomes about as popular as a snake at a sewing circle party. Dr. Connick has said,

The compulsion to correct others, coupled with complacency about one's own faults, Jesus calls hypocrisy. Reformation should be a home-grown product. Certain it is that Mr. Log-Eye is in no position to help Mr. Speck-Eye until he has had a log-rolling session with himself.

It is so easy, in criticizing another, to overlook the more-than-blemishes in ourselves. This sort of one-sided appraisal has a great effect upon us. Dr. Connick goes on to say:

> The judge is affected by his judgments. If he paints the world in purple and black, the world will thunder back at him. If he moves "on guard," he will be guarded against. If he impugns the motives of others, his motives will be questioned. If he says "Good morning" to life, it will respond in kind.
>
>> He who has a thousand friends has not a friend to spare,
>> And he who has one enemy shall meet him everywhere.

It is more than passing strange that a log in our own eye never troubles us as much as the speck in the other's eye. When we live for a long time with our shortcomings, our sins, and our weaknesses, we simply become accustomed to them. As our constant roommates, they no longer bother us with their snoring. Having become accustomed to putting up with them, we no longer desire to put them out.

But these faults and failings in others are so foreign to our own particular weaknesses and obsessions that we fight them as strangers. Being quite different from our own failures, they have not become "family" with us and we try to put them out of the household of our experiences. It is so easy for us to burn up most of our righteous indignation and energy in assailing the other person's types of sins rather than in conquering and outliving or reducing our own. The Pharisee, praying haughtily, thanks God that "I am not as other men are . . ." (Luke 18:11), but never stops to think for a moment that other men might be thanking God that they are not as he is! Most of our anger is a thrust at other people's sins, not at our own. Familiarity not only breeds contempt, it more often breeds complacency with our own weaknesses and our own particular idiosyncrasies.

Censuring others will not have so large a place if we spend more time in censuring ourselves. Nagging is a habit formed on the part of one who spends little time bettering self. Our egotism is always combative and fraternalizing and must have somebody to chastise. If we spend little time chastening ourselves, we must chasten someone else. This fury must be exercised and righteous indignation must express itself. And it will—toward ourselves or toward another.

Often children bring us self-revelation. Dr. Connick tells of a contractor who said,

> When I sat down to dinner the other night I was exhausted. Everything the children did seemed wrong. Mary tried to carry on a conversation with half her dinner in her mouth. Frank kicked his little sister under the table. She wailed! The baby spilled her milk. I found myself barking commands. "Don't put so much food in your mouth at once!" "Keep those feet still!" "Watch out! That milk costs 6¢ a glass!"
>
> After dinner, I sat down to read, but not for long. The children were playing house. Frank was the father. He shouted at Mary, "Don't put so much food in your mouth!" One by one I heard my own commands repeated. I had cast my words on the water and now they were returning. I felt ashamed. I knew now what it meant to be "poor in spirit." I was painfully aware of my spiritual need.

The children had become the revealers. How often we see ourselves frankly and honestly reflected in them! Like father, like son; as mother so is her daughter—these are the parents of humility. Occurrences such as these give birth to our confession of our own need.

## XI

## Finance—A Fury or a Fellowship?

THE FIRST OF the month—what a telltale date that is!

"Well, my dear, how in the world can we save anything when you spend money the way you do?"

She retorts angrily, "Well, you take ten dollars to the grocery store and see what you bring back in a little paper bag."

"Just the same, this has to stop."

"Well, you tell me how to stop it!" And she leaves the kitchen weeping.

There it is—the bombing of the bills, and the fury of finance. The momentary maelstrom can wreck a home if we are not careful. Peace will only come with a well-thought-out program of finance. Over many a broken home could be hung this sign: "Until Debt Do Us Part."

The monetary demands upon a couple's life today can be crushing. The first of these burdens lies in the height of our demands and desires. Someone has said, humorously or factually, that the young husband-to-be fifty years ago faced some 119 wants in his future home, of which just 17 were absolute necessities. But today he faces 973 wants, of which 117

## FINANCE—A FURY OR A FELLOWSHIP?

are absolute necessities—glass shower-doors, electric washers and dryers, garbage disposals, a TV set, a radio, and probably a hi-fi set; a tape recorder for his documents, for the recording of her favorite music or for registering for posterity the baby's gurgles; her hair-dos and his golf clubs, a car or possibly a second car, memberships, teas, dues, socials—everything that goes with "keeping up with the Joneses." Keeping face socially and keeping solvent financially are difficult partners. We have been brainwashed by commercial advertising until we feel that all these things are necessary to living.

A man said to his psychiatrist, "I have one of the most beautiful homes in Hollywood. I have a chauffeured Cadillac, two swimming pools (one for the children), a helicopter to take me to the beach club, we belong to an exclusive golf club; I man a yacht with a crew of six, and eat so well my Diner's Club bill averages more than $1000 a month."

"Under those conditions," the psychiatrist said, "what kind of a problem could you have?"

"My problem," said the patient, "is that I only make $50.00 a week."

A bizarre story, of course, but it has its practical implications. Many a wife prods her husband into keeping up with the Joneses when this process is far beyond both his creative and financial capacities.

Christ said, ". . . a man's life consisteth not in the abundance of the things which he possesseth" (Luke 12:15). We have been made to think that *things* make the home, that the way to a happy marriage is to surround ourselves with a great department store full of gadgets, and that the happiness of the marriage relationship so much depends upon how much time we spend with other people. Life is something more than just a parade in which we put on a show.

It is more a purposeful partnership in which we take on responsibilities that are thrilling and worthwhile. We must learn a captaining of inordinate desires. Our main problem today is not the "high cost of living" so much as "the cost of high living." The fact that we have a higher standard of living than our fathers certainly can be one of the facets of progress. But on the other hand, when we overdo it, it can be also one of the facets of extreme and dangerous overreaching in the realm of spending.

For protection and guidance here we need a great fundamental principle. It is the "principle of the first column." Now, the first column in many a home is entitled "What Are We Spending For?" Here are many entries—lounging jacket, Ping-pong table, beverages, food, rent, dog, medical expenses, etc. This column, of course, has its place, but it is really column #2, and should be preceded by another more important consideration. Column #1 really should be entitled "What Are We Living For?" How can we possibly determine what we shall spend our money for until we realize what we are living for?

Let us take a few examples. Suppose a young couple at the end of the month have $25 they don't know how to spend (of course, this could not happen —it is a mere supposition). He says, "Well, here's $25. What shall we do with it? How about my lounging jacket now?"

But she may reply, "In the column 'What Are We Living For?' certainly would be 'companionship with our children.' How about getting the Ping-pong table so we can spend more time with them?" You see the enlistment of the word "companionship" under the column "What Are We Living For?" determines whether or not they should buy the lounging jacket, listed under column #2, "What Are We Spending

For?" In this case, the primary purpose would take the lead over some pleasurable gadget.

But say they had $15 left. "Now is the time to get the bull pup," she might say.

He might reply, "Well, remember what the minister said about the tremendous need of foreign missions in this hour of fluid decision. Perhaps we had better put a little more in there."

"What Are We Living For?" in this case took the precedence over what they were spending for. Now, there is nothing the matter with a bull pup—but when it gets in the way of a program, it is serious. I know some young couples who spend more in a month for dog food than they give to missions in thirty days! You wouldn't believe that a couple could get things that mixed up, would you? But it is possible to lose one's sense of the vital in days like these.

The difficulty with this lack of a spiritual principle in finance lies in the fact that we do not realize what happens when we do not ". . . seek first his kingdom and his righteousness . . ." (Matthew 6:33). The minute we allow the spiritual and the missionary to go by the boards, we begin to pay for it in a very definite way. The world chaos today, much of it, grows out of the fact that the human soul has not come to any sort of maturity. We simply did not heed Christ when He said: "Go therefore and make disciples of all nations, baptizing them in the name of the Father, and of the Son, and of the Holy Spirit" (Matthew 28:19). We even forgot that this was a wise thing— the most spiritual and the most economical thing that we could do. If we do not go in missions, of course, we go in terms of the military. It costs $5,000 a year to send a missionary abroad, but many times that to send a Marine abroad—and it may cost him his dear life. When a husband, and sometimes his wife, pay for their smoking bill three times as much as people give to God for this sort of work, then they may well open the papers and see how villages and churches and homes "go up in smoke" far across the sea because of their neglect. Someone suggested before the Pacific War that if we did not send many more missionaries and teachers to Japan, we would have to send soldiers instead. We did not do the former and so of course we did the latter. This was a very expensive mistake.

Financial considerations are important before marriage as well as after. Cupid has been called a terrible liar because he merely suggests that you put your hand on your pulse to see if it is racing. But somehow he does not answer the monetary perplexities that sometimes strike the young couple as they go wide-eyed from the altar into the realisms of life. How much is necessary to begin a home? This depends on the couple, of course. Here father had better be consulted, because many times the early marriage is "C.O.D."—call on Dad! It is a good time to have a talk with the economist and the banker. Carpets do cost. Into this picture come such considerations as the size of his income during early married years, her willingness to work and the wisdom of it, the possibility of having a child, the realism with which they will face the financial pressures of the present day, and their willingness to live humbly for a time.

The most Scriptural and practical guard against this "fury of finance" lies in a definite, realistic principle of giving. One of the greatest principles is that of proportionate giving. God admonishes us to this in the words: "Upon the first day of the week let every one of you lay by him in store, as God hath prospered him . . ." (I Corinthians 16:2). You can divide this admonition into certain clear principles of saving, spending and giving. "Upon the first day of the week"—that is, giving regularly. Do not be like a faucet that spits and sputters; afford the Kingdom of God the steady flow of your gifts. When one brushes the hair only occasionally it is full of snarls and tangles and it is a painful process. But the more you brush it the better it feels. Giving is like that. Giving once in a while is painful, but giving regularly is a very pleasant exercise. The bills that have to do with the church and the Kingdom of God come in regularly and they have to be paid regularly. Unless the giving of its members supports it, the whole situation is upset and irregular.

"Let every one of you lay by"—in other words, save regularly. Lay aside, put aside a definite amount for God. The tithe of the Old Testament was always a "first" and not a "last." It is too dangerous to give to God what remains over, after we have fulfilled our whole necessities and desires. In this royal partnership of finance, God comes first; we should seek the Kingdom of God first and not last. In too many budgets there is no "remainder."

"As God hath prospered him"—that is a definite proportion of all we have. There are many who feel that the tithe, one tenth, is basic and minimum and more a test of our honesty than of our liberality. There is a difference between "tithe" and "offering." A *tithe* is that which we pay to God in interest, in recognition that the other nine tenths is His as well but that He is allowing us to use it. The *offering* is that amount between the tenth and the sum total, which will vary according to the person's earning ability, his possessions, his love and devotion.

This whole matter of proportionate giving is something more than simply a gimmick for getting money for charitable and religious purposes. It is a godly principle and as such is deeply religious. We instinctively learn to love those things to which we give and for which we work. Where our treasure is, there are our hearts also. This is a form of dedication to God and to His holy purposes.

Every home that is well run financially and spiritually needs a motive, a method, and a management. The *motive* is to seek first the Kingdom of God. The *method* is regular giving—to the proper place, person, position, or thing. And finally, *management* is the management of both our desires and our dollars —our persons and our possessions. With these factors, any financial partnership can be a fellowship instead of a fury.

# XII
# The Soul Needs Bread

THE HUSBAND AND father of a family is face to face with the battle for bread, and most of the pressures that are upon him, in his profession or in the market place, have to do with the support of his hearthside. In these struggles and pressures he best demonstrates God, who is, after all, the great Provider of all.

The father is more than the winner of bread, however. God has said, "For the husband is the head of the wife as Christ is the head of the church, his body, and is himself its Savior" (Ephesians 5:23). He has very definite spiritual obligations toward his children. The home is something more than a wild animal circus and faith is quite as important as food. And the soul is even more important than the physical aspect of the household, important as that is. As Thielicke says,

What is wrong with the kind of parental love that concentrates wholly on providing food and drink and clothes and education, perhaps even making great sacrifices to do so, and never gives the remotest thought to what is going on in the mind and soul of a teen-age boy ... ?

A young man before taking his own life wrote to me: "You are the only one whom I am telling what I intend to do. You can tell my parents. They will be thunderstruck. They never knew me, despite all their care for me. They think I am a real sonny-boy when I fall with gusto into my favorite food which my mother prepares so lovingly. They think they have fed me, but I am starved. They made a home for me, but I was cold and homeless."

And what does the young man say in the film "Rebel Without a Cause" . . . ? Here we are shown parents who provide their young son with every American comfort in life and quite definitely give a lot of thought to the question of what they can do and expend to promote his physical welfare and qualify him to meet life. But they are quite unaware of what is absorbing and engrossing him. And when he bursts out with the dreadful stress in his life and his unanswered questions, his father says to him, "Just wait, in ten years all that will be over. Then you will think differently about it." But the youth cries out, "I want to know now, *now!* And right now, when I need it, you don't have an answer for me. With all your love you simply let me down. And when I need help, when I'm in despair, you furnish me with exactly nothing." With these words he leaps at his father's throat, chokes him, and then disappears in misery.

Do these parents, or any other of these solicitous providers really love? Are they not merely abreacting their maternal and paternal feelings? And in doing so, are they not really leaving those entrusted to them to their own solitude? Are they not abandoning them to suicide, to the fate of weaklings, or to inner or actual vagabondage? And when the catastrophe comes (though in many cases it never goes that far) they stand in court completely bewildered: "I denied myself cigars and food and vacations for him. I dressed like a scarecrow in order to see that he was well dressed. But the mind and soul of my child was always a blank spot on the map of my life; I never really knew him at all."

In a technological age, on all sides we see the failure to be adequate spiritually. I was giving a week of lectures at a certain guided missile base some time ago, and one of the scientists said something like this: "You see my chief problem is not scientific. It is spiritual. I have solved the problems of fission, but I cannot solve the problem of my marriage. She is going to divorce me next month. I can control a bomb, but I cannot handle my boy. My chief trouble is not with atomic 'fallout' but with human 'fallout' —husband with wife, father with son. God help me." That is the new scientific mind in many quarters, technologically able but spiritually bankrupt. Our statistics from here on must have more to do with the human equation. Is it failing?

A man who was tending the salmon ladders in our great Northwest on one of its majestic rivers, said, "We did not lose a salmon last year!" Would that the cities of that particular state could say the same thing about their boys: "We did not lose a boy last year!" Every time a boy goes wrong, a good man dies—and there are too many casualties in the United States of America!

# XIII
# Spiritualizing Sex

THERE ARE TWO dangers in the appraisal of the importance of physical conditions in the marriage relationship. One is overemphasis, the other is underemphasis.

In the bracket of years that are just past we have had an almost inordinate emphasis upon the physical facets of marriage. Someone has said it will always be "sex o'clock" on the campus and that is quite normal. Sex has a definite place in human life but it must not be overemphasized. More books are written now on sex and sex psychology than ever before in history—and never did we suffer from so many broken homes. This used to be almost the sole approach to the marital problem, but now we realize it is only fragmentary and a part of it. We must look farther than mere "sex appeal" as a foundation on which to build a happy marriage. Real feminine beauty is far more than something that is skin deep.

James Montgomery Flagg, the famous painter, said,

> Having painted thousands of women, I do not undervalue physical beauty; but without certain feminine qualities of spirit, such beauty is a grass-cheap thing. These qualities are, in the order named: serenity, kindness, courage, humor, and passion. . . . Endowed with this vitality, women glow with an incandescence of spirit that can be felt, if not actually seen. Flesh uninhabited by spirit tends to deteriorate with appalling rapidity.

"Miss America" and "Mrs. America" are not chosen now for mere physical beauty. They are also chosen from the standpoint of proficiency in the art of conversation, a certain spiritual idealism, a knowledge of the arts and the social graces. It is only this balanced *composite* that gives to a woman her vital charm.

When Christ said, "Wilt thou be made whole?" (John 5:6), He was making His offer to the whole, well-rounded and balanced personality. This, of course, will include the physical emotions as well as spiritual qualities.

Frigidity, emotional inabilities, have had their vital part in destroying many a marriage. Religion comes in here to aid. A reading of I Corinthians 7 will at least begin to emphasize the beauty of this marriage relationship in God's sight and the place that it should have in the life of the married couple. To shy away from this is not to be spiritual, it is merely to be peculiar. It is not to be pure so much as it is to be prudish. The marriage relationship should result in the highest sort of communion, the deepest nearness that two can experience. To fail in this facet of the marriage contract is to fail pathetically. One man said, "I should sue my wife for non-emotional support." This is as bad an insufficiency, of course, as lack of financial support and is pathetic when it is seen on either side of the marriage. It is possible for us to become adequate in this way and we should study to do so. Here is a field of nearness or departure. Let us get this right at the start—as human beings we are both body and spirit and we must function as such.

There is nothing unholy about the physical marriage relationship, for this is a God-established thing. Christ said, "The two shall become one flesh [as well as spirit] . . ." (Mark 10:8), and when He said *flesh*, He meant it: bodily one. No couple has worked out its whole strategy until it is cared for in this. There is a difference between love and lust—the lust is simply physical desire without any spiritual quality. Someone has said, "Purity is not abstinence or denial of passion. It is just the rightful ordering of feeling." This physical union has been blessed of God, and the lack of it has God's frown. Oscar Watkins said, "The highest and most intimate of spiritual relationships can never be marriage without the union of flesh."

To be inadequate emotionally is a severe failure, whether it be on the part of either husband or wife, and there are usually reasons for it. We are born with normal desires and for one to deny the other their expression is nothing less than brutal. All this goes along with the marriage vow. When we pledge ourselves in loyalty to each other, we must never rob the other of the right that goes along with that loyalty. If one soul says, "Stay with me, be loyal to me," then that soul must also say, "I will give thee all that goes along with that loyalty." Asking loyalty one must not deny that thing that makes it easy for another to be loyal.

Inadequacy here gives birth to all sorts of upsets mentally, physically, and spiritually. Biological tensions are set up when this possible, happy relationship is not worked out. Little issues between husband and wife become gigantic tensions and they make mountains out of molehills, just because they are not living naturally.

Skirting some of the physical reasons for frigidity, let us mention some of the spiritual bases for it. One leading expert claims that frigidity in marriage is on the increase because spirituality is on the decrease;

but what has frigidity to do with spirituality? A great deal. He goes on to say that to many a man the marriage relationship is merely a means of achieving a result, while to the woman it is more a sense of spirit, how she feels toward her husband—her devotion, her admiration, her inner sense of spirit. Whatever causes a woman to be upset mentally, or to be disappointed spiritually, will cause her to be chilled emotionally. Why is this? Because marriage is not the mating of two bodies alone; it is also the mating of two souls and the soul must work with the body.

There is a sense in which marriage is a three-story affair. There is a third floor of the spiritual where we worship together, where we appreciate God together, where we pray together. If we disagree here, a certain disunity will seep down into the second floor, which is our emotional and mental state. This will lead us to disputes, mental and intellectual debating and haggling; and this division on the second floor naturally seeps down into the physical relations of the first floor and takes the deepest desire from them. Everything that is crowned, is crowned from above! Unless in the marriage relationship there is an "above," some spiritual rapport, it is difficult for the physical relationship to be at its best.

So much of the satisfactory physical life is based on an unselfish principle: "Let the husband render unto the wife due benevolence . . ." (I Corinthians 7:3). This is the type of unselfish thoughtfulness and deference to be practiced. ". . . and likewise also the wife unto the husband" (I Corinthians 7:3). What "benevolence"? Well, this is part of it: "The wife does not rule over her own body, but the husband does; likewise the husband does not rule over his own body, but the wife does" (I Corinthians 7:4). The husband should give to the wife her conjugal rights and likewise the wife to her husband: "Do not refuse one another . . . lest Satan tempt you through lack of self-control" (I Corinthians 7:5). The devil has a fine chance to make an entrance into life when we do not satisfy each other's sexual needs.

It is plain here that God commands a married couple to be considerate of each other's wish—more of the wish of the other than of one's own desire. One should not deny the other, save for a good reason, and let us be sure it is good! If this consideration is not practiced, then Satan enters and brings with him every type of confusion and upset, causing one or the other to stumble.

Amber Blanco White says that "to be indifferent to the physical expressions of love, still more to dislike it, or to feel that it is in some way shameful, is neither superior nor virtuous nor refined; it is a symptom of mental illness, or maladjustment." Let us remember that purity is not prudery, and chastity is not emotional inadequacy. Good lovers must be good partners, and good partners must be good lovers or they fail. God would make us adequate here. When Jesus Christ said to the sick man, "Wilt thou be made whole? . . ." (John 5:6), He was asking, "Will you be made well rounded, lacking nothing?" This is Christ's gift and it should be His gift to us in the realm of the physical.

## XIV
## Adjusting Ourselves to Each Other

LET US FACE IT: in marriage we begin as twain, we are two personalities. Our backgrounds have done things to us whether we are conscious of it or not and we bring these effects, these harvests of the personality, into our marriage and into our home. There troop along behind us habit patterns—our friendships, our ways of thinking, and our dispositional peculiarities.

First of all, we are male and female—and because of this we normally think differently, feel differently, and are impressed by or seek out different things. When we have learned that, we do not let it upset or discourage us. It is God's way of giving alternate beats to the same heart of a home; yet there can result a oneness. These differences therefore should not make us despair, but should challenge us to start understanding each other, preferring one another, adjusting ourselves to each other. Someone has said, "You can never expect the wages of happiness without working for them."

Many times people say, "We are different, that is all." We may thank God for that—it means we might borrow the best from each other. When people who are married have different characteristics, each can share with the other, thus enlarging and enriching their lives; if they were both of the same type, they would merely overemphasize their peculiarities and idiosyncrasies and become more severely typed. One may be an introvert and like to stay home in the evening, love to pore over books, do some deep ruminating and have fellowship with the TV. If the hearthside is the most welcome place at eventide, because one is tired of the world, one naturally looks for the opportunity to undress the soul. But if, on the other hand, the other is an extrovert and wants to dress for dinner, loves people, friendships, loves the thrill of activity and a friendly going about, this one too has something to contribute to the partnership.

Here is an opportunity, now, for "give and take." Let the extrovert who likes to be active spend some time in quietness, learn more about good books, and the art of conversation. Let that one go deep. On the other hand, let the introvert go out to meet people, to realize the value of a social world, the church family, and to laugh with them. "A cheerful heart is a good medicine . . ." (Proverbs 17:22).

Here, both the husband and the wife can move toward each other. And both must move. Two introverts make recluses; two extroverts make gadabouts. Each is good for the other, but they must meet at the center, at a point of balance. Let us not cry out stubbornly, "Move over to where I am." In honor we must prefer one another, give in to each other. This is character, not weakness. This is a sign of unselfish strength.

The Master said, "If any man will come after me, let him *deny himself*, and take up his cross, and follow me" (Matthew 16:24). The crucifixion of self is one of the most difficult but thrilling secrets of the Christian life. It is very hard on stubborn pride. It is very difficult for any of us to admit we need anything from the other. Dr. C. G. Jung said: "Seldom, or perhaps never, does a marriage develop into an individual relationship smoothly and without crisis; there is no coming to consciousness without pain." And

one of the deepest pains in life is crucifixion of self—
nailing it to the cross of a higher purpose than ourselves. It is so hard to die to self. Very few can honestly say: "I have been crucified with Christ, it is no longer I who live, but Christ who lives in me . . ." (Galatians 2:20). This displacement of self by another is hard, but one of the most vital techniques of married life.

Quarrels will occur in a marriage, more for some than others, but there is no finality in this. A broken bone may be stronger than before the breakage, if it heals properly. But self on center utterly spoils the healing; for the process is never handled happily by God until self abdicates in a healthy manner.

Martin Luther once said, "Between husband and wife there should be no question between *Me-um* and *Te-um* [mine and thine]." All things should be in common between them without any distinction, or means of distinguishing. It is this battle between "me" and "thee" that becomes so destructive; and may we repeat that until Christ conquers *both* of us, we will both go on trying to conquer each other, and that will be war at its most miserable and at its worst.

"Seekest thou great things for thyself? seek them not . . ." (Jeremiah 45:5). For self on center, self on the throne is paganism. Christianity is self dethroned, and Christ taking over; self decreasing, while Christ is increasing; self becoming silent, while Christ is speaking—until self becomes nothing and Christ becomes everything. This is living! Everything else is merely existing.

What a battle! D. L. Moody said: "The man I have more trouble with than anybody else is D. L. Moody." This is our common problem. Sometimes self is so enthroned that we cannot even rejoice in the victory of another; not even in the success of a

## ADJUSTING OURSELVES TO EACH OTHER

friend, or a cause—if it seemingly is not our success. We are simply flat when we try to join in another's song of victory. If marriage fails, it is due more to the concept that the other has failed us, than that we have failed the other. Self-pity can become as obnoxious as cheap perfume and some people douse themselves with it! They are caught up in a little world filled with their own problems, their own heartaches, their own accomplishments, and they have been blinded somehow to the outside world—its hearts, its songs, its sighs, its victories and its needs. No pyramid can stand upon its narrow apex; it tumbles over. No life can stand when it is built upon self; it just topples.

There is but one cure here: the utter surrender of our hearts to Jesus Christ. The displacement of self by the Spirit, the subordinating of our own needs to the needs of others. This was Jesus Christ, this was His artistry. They said to Him on the cross, "He saved others, he cannot save himself" (Mark 15:31), and they thought it was an insult. This was the greatest honor ever paid to any man. These are the laws of God. Others first and self second, and any reversal of the process is putting the cart before the horse, and ends either in the ditch or in no progress.

It has made Theodore Monod write these searching lines:

> Oh, the bitter shame and sorrow
>   That a time could ever be
> When I let the Saviour's pity
> Plead in vain, and proudly answered,
>   "All of self and none of Thee."
>
> Yet He found me; I beheld Him!
>   Bleeding on the accursed tree;
> Heard Him pray, "Forgive them, Father";

And my wistful heart said faintly,
   "Some of self and some of Thee.'

Day by day, His tender mercy,
   Healing, helping, full and free,
Sweet and strong, and oh, so patient,
Brought me lower, while I whispered,
   "Less of self, and more of Thee."

Higher than the highest heavens,
   Deeper than the deepest sea,
Lord, Thy love at last has conquered·
Grant me now my soul's desire,
   "None of self and all of Thee."

There are three types of lives. One is to live for self, with self first in all considerations. This is a respectable sin—but a dangerous one.

Secondly, life can be a partnership in which we honor the rights of others as well as our own. There is a subtle temptation here, however, to keep things in balance. We have our own rights as well as others, and we must see that we get at least our 50 per cent of devotion and consideration. Eye for eye, and tooth for tooth, marriage is a 50-50 proposition, and we become quite irritated if we do not get our half. We apologize for this by calling it inherent justice and a balance in the scale of demands. This, too, can be treacherous.

The third principle of life is living for others primarily, ". . . in honour preferring one another" (Romans 12:10). That is, giving the other the preference. Life is not asking merely what it receives; it is fascinated with what it can give. It is more interested in the outgo than in the intake. Its passion now is not so much to be loved, but to be loving. This is such certain release from egoism; this is the slaughter of egocentrism. Christ challenges us to it when He says,

"If any man will come after me, let him deny himself . . ." (Matthew 16:24). This is the royal filling: emptied of ourselves, we are filled with Christ. God give us grace so to deny ourselves and follow Him! Then we shall find that the crucifixion of self is always followed by exaltation and glorification at the right hand of God!

## XV
## Thankfulness and Thoughtfulness

"LOVE IS FRIENDSHIP SET TO MUSIC." It is quite up to us to increase the orchestration or to throttle down the harmony—and it is easy for us just to go along, allowing another's kindnesses to pass unappreciated, his deeds to be unsung.

We have a choice to make—in our daily tasks we can believe we are drinking from golden chalices of privilege or from the brazen cups of mundane duty. We must not allow life to become ordinary. It would be a splendid thing if we could carry the appreciation and ready praise and thoughtfulness of the engagement days on through the years that follow. It is a long cry sometimes from the day in which he helped her from the automobile as though she were a Cinderella on her way to the ball, and the day on which, at his wife's delayed departure, he called out, "Oh, get a move on, darling, shake a leg!"

There are certain subtle decays, subtle discourtesies, that can creep into married life and we must be on guard against them. There is never any excuse for husband and wife not treating each other as gentleman and lady. There will always be a certain etiquette to marriage and we must do all we can to keep the household royal in its conduct and attitudes. The corsage, the box of candy, and the bouquet of flowers should never be strange to the hearthside of today. It is so easy for us to take love for granted and cease to festoon it with the niceties that give it rightful charm.

A wife's whole day and a husband's whole day can be tremendously characterized by the mood in which they part after breakfast. The quiet prayer, the Scripture reading, the word of praise can be like oil in the machinery, to keep the bearings from freezing in the mad mechanics of modern living.

We wield the brushes of disposition and atmosphere, and we splash the color of the paints of our personality upon others who live near us. Our loved one goes out just as naturally, taking the color of our own feelings—despondency, or happiness, a sigh or a song, defeat or victory. Katherine Pinkerton has said "If one must leave a home, a ship, or a woman, leave should be taken while one is still in love." All our leave-takings, if but for a few hours or for days or months, should be taken in love. This is the only adequate launching pad from which to go out to perform daily tasks and meet daily problems. It is this loving send-off that gives the thrust we need in the orbits of life.

> If I had known in the morning
> How wearily all the day
>     The words unkind
>     Would trouble my mind
> I said when you went away,
> I had been more careful, darling,
>     Nor given you needless pain;
> But we vex our own

> With look and tone
>> We might never take back again.
>
> For though in the quiet evening
> You may give me the kiss of peace,
>> Yet it might be
>> That never for me
> The pain of the heart should cease.
> How many go forth in the morning
>> That never come home at night,
> And hearts have broken
> For harsh words spoken
>> That sorrow can ne'er set right.
>
> We have careful thoughts for the stranger,
> And smiles for the sometime guest.
>> But oft for our own
>> The bitter tone,
> Though we love our own the best.
> Oh, lips with the curve impatient,
>> And brow with that look of scorn,
> 'Twere a cruel fate
> Were the night too late
>> To undo the work of the morn.

# XVI
# Spiritual Oneness

MARRIAGE IS NOT only the mating of two bodies and two minds; it is primarily the mating of two souls. "They shall not only be one in flesh, but also one in spirit" (Mark 10:8). We must never disappoint each other on this upper level of religion; no let-down is so serious in married life as one discovering the spiritual inadequacy of the other.

A woman has a great deal to do with her husband's spiritual development. One man said to me, "Were it not for the church and my wife I would have gone to pieces long ago under the bludgeonings of my problems." In order to be to him what a wife should be, she must dig her spiritual wells to great depths that he may draw from them in hours of spiritual drought which come to every man under the pressures of the modern day. When Job asked his wife what he should do in his straitened circumstances—when he had lost cattle, servants, house and sons—he received the reply: "Do you still hold fast to your integrity? Curse God, and die" (Job 2:9). Imagine the disappointment in being married to a woman whose life was stuffed, like a child's doll, with sawdust; a woman without spiritual depth or sources of comfort, or wellsprings of courage!

The Bible says that we should serve the Lord with godly *fear*. ". . . let us offer to God acceptable worship, with reverence and awe" (Hebrews 12:28). What sort of fear is this? It is in essence not the fear that God should hurt us, but the fear that we might hurt God by failing to fulfill His high expectations of us. The "godly fear" with which husband and wife are to look upon each other, and upon themselves, is not the fear that one might harm the other, but rather the fact that one, by falling short, might disappoint the other.

Men will always find it difficult to live up to the highest ideal set by a wifely affection. But the climb must be attempted and the heights must be scaled, at least in part. Of course, such spiritual maturity in a man is not easily come upon. Someone has said, "The only difference between a man and a boy is that a man's toys cost more." And it is quite easy for us even in the mature world to continue to speak as a child, understand as a child, and think as a child. It is difficult for us, even when men, to "put away childish things."

> Lord, may there be no moment in her life
> When she regrets that she became my wife,
> And keep her dear eyes just a trifle blind
> To my defects, and to my failings, kind!
>
> Help me to do the utmost that I can
> To prove myself her measure of a man,
> But, if I often fail as mortals may,
> Grant that she never sees my feet of clay!
>
> And let her make allowance—now and then
> That we are only grown-up boys, we men,
> So, loving all our children, she will see,
> Sometimes, a remnant of the child in me!

# XVII
# The Head of the House

WHO IS TO TAKE the spiritual leadership of the home? Someone has said, "The husband is the head of the house, but the wife is the heart of the home." If that be true, certainly these are co-partners in giving the home its dignity and its power.

Paul does say, ". . . the husband is the *head* of the wife" (Ephesians 5:23). Christ also reminds us that ". . . they twain shall be one . . ." (Mark 10:8). One man who quoted this quite proudly exclaimed, "We two are one, my dear, and *I am that one!*" Now there are some men, of course, who view the marriage relationship as a certificate printed on pink paper, in the likeness of a slip of ownership. But the wedding certificate is printed on white paper of partnership. The woman's state is one not so much of subordination as one of creative partnership. Her husband does not "own her," he "loves her."

Of course, a man is expected under God, to assume a certain leadership in the home. The husband is the head of the wife, and the average woman, we believe, rejoices to see a dynamic leadership on the part of the man of the house. Of course, a man must earn this position of leadership. When Paul says that the man is "head of the wife," there is a qualification: he is the head of the wife ". . . as Christ is the head of the church" (Ephesians 5:23).

How did Christ become *head* of the church? By following definitely the will of God. Christ said, "My meat is to do the will of him that sent me, and to finish his work" (John 4:34); and that ". . . he that hath seen me hath seen the Father . . ." (John 14:9). That is, Christ brought His life into such obedience to the will of God, He took such a position as to the wish and pattern of God, that when people followed Him they were at the same time following God. Now, in this way He earned the right to become the head of the church, and, of course, the church in following Christ is naturally following God.

A husband, before he can become the head of the house, must put himself in such a relationship with God—understand the will of God, follow the will of God—that when his wife is following him, he is naturally leading her to follow God. Until a man has maneuvered his life, his will, his heart into such a position, he has not earned, nor does he rate, the position as "head of the house." When he has done so, however, a wife pleasing him as her husband is automatically pleasing God. Her safeguard is the phrase found in Colossians 3:18, "in the Lord."

# THE HEAD OF THE HOUSE

The same qualification, of course, applies to the parents' leadership of the children. Paul says, "Children, obey your parents in the Lord: for this is right" (Ephesians 6:1). The qualifying phrase that attaches itself to obedience is the same: "in the Lord." That is, please your parents insofar as in pleasing the parents, you please the Lord. This is a definite limitation and qualification. Should a father admonish and command his son to aid him in robbing a bank, the son would be under no obligation to obey his father in this regard for that command would not meet the qualifying phrase or be within the compass of God's will. Every parent ought so to maneuver his or her life into line with the will of God that when the child is obeying the parent, the child is at the same time normally obeying God. No parent should ever maneuver his child into a position where he asks the child to displease God in the same act in which he is pleasing his parents.

This surrender to the will of God by which the man stands as the head of the house gives birth to certain problems when it is lacking. A woman came into my office very much upset and said: "Dr. Evans, I don't know what to do. My husband insists on seeing the double-header ball game at 1:20 every Sunday afternoon during the baseball season. That means he must eat dinner promptly at noon each Sunday. I remonstrated with him, suggesting that it is my duty to be in the house of God. He, however, has countered with this question: 'You're a Christian, aren't you?'

"To this I have replied, 'I think I am.'

"Then he says, 'Your Bible says, "Wives, be subject to your husbands," and if you are a Christian, you will obey me. Dinner every Sunday at twelve!' What shall I do?"

I said, "You go home and tell your husband that his God is his belly! He has only quoted part of that command; he forgot to say 'Wives be subject to your husbands . . . *in the Lord.*' Or, in other words, insofar as in obeying them you obey God. The husband has no right to force upon you such a schedule as will crowd God out of your day. His repast on a Sunday ought in no way to get in the way of your worship of God on that Lord's Day. He is purely out of bounds and in no position to demand this of you."

On the other hand, many a spiritual life has been threatened by the unreasonable requests of a woman. Many a man has compromised somewhat in business in order to gain the rapid success financially and socially that his wife coveted. Many a man has whittled down on matters of conscience and conduct in order that his wife might make that social whirl of her life that her heart had always strangely and intensely desired. More than one man is in jail because he took shortcuts to unreasonable gain to satisfy his wife's inordinate desire to "keep up with the Joneses."

It is true that we hold the other's soul in our hands and do mold it, very definitely. Here we must exercise supreme care to be always in the will of God, each exerting his or her own influence in line with this desire of the heavenly Father.

Many a marriage could have been saved if the couple had remembered this—that *their hearts belong to each other, but their souls belong to God!* You and I are asked to *love* each other, but we are asked to *worship* God. God must always be on *center*, as the great *first* in every home. We have no right to commandeer the soul of the other. That belongs to God; never touch it. It was this, I think, that made one partner say to another:

My soul will never, never be yours alone;
Too many things I love, to speak that lie:
Red tides of sunset breaking on the sky,
Slow twilights and the first rose bloom
To fiery splendor in a day in spring,
Cold mountain water, passionate and strong
And wild with music, and a sharp sweet song
Of birds when day has folded like a wing,
There is a love that worships God alone as King!

There is a love that unto Him alone I bring;
If you refuse Him what is His by right
How could I love thee as I might?
But bid me live for Him, then know
That I would die for thee!
Loving Him best I shall love thee the more;
And my lips will always seek your own,
But my soul can never, never be yours alone.

# XVIII
# You Mold Each Other

ONE DAY A DENTIST said to me, "I must accept Christ and join the church. I have watched my wife. When I first knew her she taught a Sunday School class, sang in the choir, and was a faithful servant of the church and of the Kingdom of God. But my secularism has gradually robbed her of these things. She no longer stands on a pedestal where she was when first I found her. I want her back there, and I want to stand with her." This is a frank confession of a man who had forgotten that he was to be the spiritual leader in the home.

So many women marry men to reform them, but if there is a sign on a bus saying "Cincinnati," that is probably where it is going. By the time a woman falls in love with a mature man it is already evident the direction he has chosen. If his mother could not change him, his wife probably cannot. As Tennyson said:

> Yet it shall be: thou shalt lower to his level
>     day by day,
> What is fine within thee growing coarse to
>     sympathize with clay.
>
> As the husband is, the wife is: thou are mated
>     with a clown,
> And the grossness of his nature will have
>     weight to drag thee down.
>
> He will hold thee, when his passion shall
>     have spent its novel force,
> Something better than his dog, a little
>     dearer than his horse.

It is thrillingly possible for a husband to encourage his wife in spiritual things. One woman said, "I grow, just reaching up to him." Every man should qualify spiritually to be a mountain climber, to scale the spiritual heights, as a good wife desires.

The devotional exercise is like a bath. It is well, morning or evening, or both, by devotion to wash off the dust of the city streets from our feet, to dissolve the petty jealousies that the day has gathered, to remove the unloveliness that has cluttered up the heart, like dust on the furniture. We must take time to dissolve the fears that corrode the soul and the sins that fester in the heart. The family clothing needs a washing no more than our souls need it. The promises of God are great cleansing streams. Our canary never sang its best until it had had its morning bath, and that can be true of our souls.

There is a sense in which the husband should

## YOU MOLD EACH OTHER

direct the domestic play. Of course, together the couple decide whether their lives are going to be of some importance. Some homes just put on a little puppet show, with the motif of cheapness, with clap-trap ideals, with cheap tinsel and small doll-talk. Their one passion is to keep up appearances or to please themselves. There are other homes whose stage is touched with lofty concepts, where there is a great plot of the Kingdom of God. Here the man should be the director of the play, though many times the wife "writes the script."

But certainly, whatever their position might be on the stage of life, this is a drama that should have the dignity of God and the lofty purpose of life. When the curtain is rung down upon their marriage at the last, there should be not only the applause of men, but the applause of God, the only sure Critic and Appraiser.

As the husband molds the wife, there is a sense in which he, too, is wet clay under the skillful hands of his marriage partner. In seeming to follow, in a way she also leads.

> As the bow unto the cord is
> So unto the man is woman
> Though she bends him, she obeys him,
> Though she draws him, yet she follows,
> Useless each without the other.

Of course, the molding of each other can include some loving correction. Too often it is called "nagging." One wife said, "What experts are paid for at the office, at the plant, in the school—that is called *nagging* in the home."

But a wife's influence on a man's life can be more affirmative and constructive than it is negative and critical. We are shaped by example more than any-

thing else. More men have been won to Jesus Christ
by a woman's demonstration than by her debate, by
her life than by some lesson she was able to teach.
There is a beautifully descriptive poem by an unknown author:

> I love you,
> Not only for what you are,
> But for what I am
> When I am with you.
>
> I love you,
> Not only for what
> You have made of yourself,
> But for what
> You are making of me.
>
> I love you
> For the part of me
> That you bring out;
> I love you
> For putting your hand
> Into my heaped-up heart
> And passing over
> All the foolish, weak things
> That you can't help
> Dimly seeing there,
> And for drawing out
> Into the light
> All the beautiful belongings
> That no one else has looked
> Quite far enough to find.
>
> I love you because you
> Are helping me to make
> of the lumber of my life
> Not a tavern
> But a temple;
> Out of the works
> Of my every day
> Not a reproach
> But a song. . . .

This sort of perfecting of another—helping of another—takes a great deal of patience. The husband will have to be patient with the wife and the wife will have to be patient with the boyish fevers and act as a nurse until they pass. There will be the temporary delirium of fascination, maybe, with someone else; there will be the boyish tears that she can help to dry and care for; the temporary emptiness that only she can fill.

So many divorced women have been too much in haste and have said to me so often, "If I had only waited!" Paul says in I Corinthians 7:13: "If any woman has a husband who is an unbeliever, and he consents to live with her, she should not divorce him. For the unbelieving husband is consecrated through his wife and the unbelieving wife is consecrated through her husband."

As a woman came into my study some years ago, distraught and heartsick, she said to me: "Pastor, I can't stand it any more—his drunken kiss on my lips, the children running from him in abject fear! I'm through. I can't take it any more!"

"All right," I replied, "let's pray to God now and tell Him that you can't take it any more."

After the prayer she looked up at me with grave face and tear-stained eyes and said, "I think I can try it for another month."

As she went out the door, I said, "Goodby, soldier. See you in a month." But we did not wait a month. Just a week later she called up and said, "It happened. He found Christ and now everything is happy as a marriage bell. The children run to meet him now, and their grades have shot up to A's. How glad I am I waited!"

Yes, how glad so many are that they wait, with the longsuffering and tenderness of God. They wait for each other, they wait for God to work. Christ is a good repairman, if we bring Him all the pieces, and also give Him time!

You and I were not married to perfection; we were married to a person. God's love for us is not because of what we are, but often in spite of what we are. Love endures as well as enjoys; it stands by as well as leaps in joy; it ". . . believes all things . . ." and seldom despairs of all things. Love is not only responding lovingly to favors done us, to the faithfulness and to the splendor that is in the other; love is also loving "in spite of," or "in the face of the lack of."

"But God shows his love for us in that while we were yet sinners Christ died for us" (Romans 5:8). Only this sort of love keeps the concrete of the hearthside together. This is the only kind of love that makes us like God, and qualifies us to live with God forever—for God is Love!

# XIX
# Forgiveness

THERE WILL ALWAYS be in our lives something to forgive and forget on the part of each concerning the other. This has become a habit with God Himself, to whom we have found it necessary to pray daily: "Forgive us our debts . . ." forgetting sometimes to add "as we forgive our debtors."

Dr. Connick has said,

> God's forgiveness is not limited *to* our forgiving; it is only limited *by* it. . . . Forgiving spirits are urgently

needed. They help turn foes into friends, lawsuits into love feasts, and neighborhood feuds into neighborhood fun. What a pity so many of us practice General Oglethorpe's philosophy. He remarked to John Wesley, "I never forgive." With characteristic candor and cogency, Wesley replied, "Then I hope, sir, you never sin."

We must be as ready swiftly to use forgiveness for the other's sin against us as God is willing to use His in our sin against Him. Unforgiveness in our hearts separates us from God.

A husband had prayed long and laboriously, with blood and sweat and tears. Finally his prayer was answered. He went to his personal safe and took out a sheaf of letters. Here was costly evidence against her loyalties—evidence that might have set him free. They had been held in the dismal safe of a sour heart, but God had forgiven him his own transgressions and now he was willing to cast hers into the fire, and remember them no more. As the evidence went up in smoke, as he saw disappearing before him all means of "getting even"; as he saw there consumed the whip that had been held in his hand, the weapon that could destroy, he saw these condemning things transformed into ashes. The ashes of forgiveness! Then peace came, as God has promised. There is no possibility of our enjoying completely the lavishness of God's forgiveness of us until we have learned to be just as lavish in our forgiveness of those who have offended us. *This is a reciprocal thing, this peace of mind and heart.* Till we are willing to allow others the forgiveness that He allows us, we have lost the peace of God.

> If an unkind word appears,
> File the thing away.
> If some novelty endears,
> File the thing away.

> If some clever little bit
> Of a sharp and pointed wit
> Carrying a sting with it,
> File the thing away.
>
> If some bit of gossip come,
> File the thing away.
> Scandalously spicy crumb,
> File the thing away.
>
> If suspicion comes to you,
> If your neighbor isn't true,
> Let me tell you what to do,
> File the thing away.
>
> Do this for a little while
> Then go and burn the file.

Here is a recipe for a great deal of happiness, a prescription for many a broken heart: ". . . forgiving one another as God in Christ forgave you" (Ephesians 4:32). All of us will run upon many an opportunity to exercise this Christian grace of forgiveness and long-suffering within our homes and at our hearthsides. For ". . . all have sinned and fall short of the glory of God" (Romans 3:23). And this is true in thought, in word, and in deed. We shall have to learn the constant use of this Christian grace and attribute of character, if marriage is to survive. This is a very legitimate prayer: "Oh, God, give us a little to forgive each other each day, that we may grow in the nature and character and long-suffering of God."

An apology is so often considered a sign of weakness, whereas in reality it is a sign of strength. It is more difficult, sometimes, to confess our weaknesses or to parade our faults in the face of those whom we most dearly love than in the presence of anyone else. This may be a recoiling from any chance of destroy-

# FORGIVENESS

ing the other's respect for us. It may also simply be ego in its proudest parade.

The problem will always arise here as to whom to confess our sins.

They must be confessed to God, of course. There is ". . . one mediator between God and men, the man Christ Jesus" (I Timothy 2:5), and He is the constant, and adequate, and dependable recipient of any recital of our weaknesses or our sins, our short-comings, our omissions, or our commissions.

But how about confessing our sins to others? ". . . if you are offering your gift at the altar, and there remember that your brother has something against you, leave your gift there before the altar and go; first be reconciled to your brother, and then come and offer your gift" (Matthew 5:23-24). Now there are some things that we can constructively "patch up" by going to the enemy and not waiting for the enemy to come to us. There are some situations that can be righted. Gossiping stories can be followed by a courageous retraction; there are apologies that ought to be asked for; there may be a restitution of money stolen.

Of course many of these things are beyond our recovering. One day a woman came to her pastor and said, "Pastor, I gossiped against a friend. It was a most horrible thing I said. What can I do?"

He said, "Go out into a field and take a ripened thistle blossom. Cast the feathery parts of it into the furrows of the ploughed field."

This she did and came back to him. "What shall I do further?"

"Go back now and gather them all up."

"This is quite impossible," she said.

Then he replied, "So it is impossible to cover words or recover them, carelessly spoken. The seeds have been sown. They will bring their harvest." That is the tragic character of some of our sins—they are beyond our recovery.

Let us confess our sins *to God*—some should be for Him alone. I think there is a principle here that can be adhered to: always limit the conflagration of the flame of sin; do not hurt by confession any more people than you must.

A second principle is this: do not trust human nature—trust God. There are many people who do not have the capacities for being spiritual confidants, nor are they adequate, in their propensities of forgiveness and forgetting, to qualify as the recipients of confession.

There was a young man with a happy family, a wife and children, who suddenly felt the need for a "confessional catharsis." In such an atmosphere and under such an urge he told his wife that during one of the World Wars he had had relations with two French girls in Paris. He thought he should "get this off his chest." The wife was unable to accept the blow, and committed suicide by taking poison. She was not spiritually capable of being a confidant. She could not "play God" and forgive and forget. Often this is asking too much of human nature. A gushing, thoughtless confession can destroy rather than mend.

I think that when we speak of sin we should always ask certain questions. First of all, why do we want to tell it? Is it for a selfish reason? In the second place, will it make other people happy or will it simply add sorrow and put a burden upon others? Third, will it help the situation, righting wrongs and bettering relationships?

If our confessions pass through the gates of these questions, they are likely to approach sanity, thoughtfulness and prudence. Much heartache has been caused by the loose tongue, by careless speech, by an overestimation of the human heart and its capacity to remit sins, to give atonement, and to rightly forget. There is such a thing as "speaking the truth in love" and there is such a thing as speaking truth in utter lovelessness and brutality.

There are people who find satisfaction in dealing with the bizarre, the lecherous, and the questionable. Like garbage pails, they are always open to receive the refuse of human action. They are always encouraging people to come out with their "story" which they consume with ungodly appetite and satisfaction. God has said, "But immorality and all impurity or covetousness must not even be named among you, as is fitting among saints" (Ephesians 5:3). Our conversations should be as elevating as possible. As Paul has admonished us: "Finally, brethren, whatever is true, whatever is honorable, whatever is just, whatever is pure, whatever is lovely, whatever is gracious, if there is any excellence, if there is anything worthy of praise, think about these things" (Philippians 4:8).

There have been some "confessional cults" that have specialized in hearing and sharing the bizarre of life; these groups have given birth to a great many pathetic results in this disintegration of the personality, when they should have been halted by the application of the wisest of our spiritual principles.

Let us ask forgiveness of those who in such participation have been injured, and of God, who is ever hurt by our transgression. Let us be careful not to enlarge the circle of the injured or to bring unjust sorrow upon those whose peace we could so easily destroy.

While this whole problem has many ramifications, I think it is well to remember some of these principles that have been reiterated here. God is a God of forgiveness, restoration and repair. His hands know this artistry, of which the average human heart and human hands fall so far short. In His forgiveness, in His ability to receive us as we are, we may have full confidence.

# XX
# The Church and the Home

LOVE HAS A LOCALE—it is called "home." Here it most deeply expresses itself; here it most truly receives its nourishment and radiates its powers. So our love for God has its dwelling place, its locale and its home. It is the church and we should all find our place in it.

If you are joined at its altars in marriage and its kiss of blessing is on your brow, then, as statistics show, your marriage will have many times more chance of being a happy one than if the ceremony were performed by a civil magistrate or secular officer. When the child comes, the church will help you dedicate it to God as the Pilot, as, with its little three-inch sail, it is launched on the great sea of life; when the heat of life's midday toil and pressure is hot upon you, you find the church to be a "rock in a weary land" and its coolness and shade are God's gift to you. When sickness comes, the church will teach you how to reach out and "touch the hem of His garment" and be whole again; or, when comes the smell of funeral flowers, the church will teach you how to dry your tears on the white pages of its promises and rise to greet Death simply as a white-robed porter who has come to open the door of the Father's House to let your loved one in. It will help you walk together through life's calm and storm, and in the end will have done more than any other institution to help you stand together in life's twilight, still hand in hand, still very proud, still thanking God so much for each other.

Remember this: with money you can build a house; add love to that house and you have a home; add God to that home and you have a temple. And may we never forget that, made in the image of God as we all are, we shall never live at our happiest or at our highest until home is a temple.

Then when death comes, and one lays the other in God's arms, heaven will not seem far away or strange —the hearthside shall have been a touch of heaven!

# XXI
# Keep Yourselves From Idols

IN THE ARCHITECTURAL drawings for the place called "home," make no provision for "shrines for idols." Niches for strange gods have no place in the happy dwelling place of God's people.

What is a "god"? A man's "god" is whatever and whoever comes first in his life and reckoning. It is that force or individual that challenges the right of God within him, that in the final sense determines his choices, makes his decisions and weighs more heavily in his time, strength and considerations than all else. Therefore the "god" of any household may be anything—health, wealth, position, acceptance in the social order, popularity, praise, glory, or self. It may be "the God and Father of our Lord Jesus Christ" who is the only true "God"—the great first.

It takes a clever and keen, honest mind to ferret out the truth as to what our main, magnificent obsession really is. Who or what truly wears the crown? These other "gods," these subtle "firsts" that creep into our lives and take their places quietly in the shrines of our true devotions are numerous in their possibilities.

There is the idol of *self*. This enthronement of self may start early; even in the early nursing period of life we may become tyrants slowly but surely. The lack of parental discipline, the wheedling of our desires from weak parental withstanding, the crying and screaming into fruition of our childish desires, the resultant domination of the group of youngsters in the play-yard, the absurd freedom that sometimes results from the lazy parental mind that tires of "arguing" and coming to grips with adolescent wills, the triumph of the childish tantrum, the bullying our way through life—all these unrestricted and uncontrolled growths of our ego begin to enthrone self on the altars of our hearts. Once enthroned, the dislodgment of this false god of self is most difficult—the gigantic god-idol Dagon was not more securely entrenched or fixed on its pedestal. Some devoted tutors endeavor to dethrone this demagogue. The patient schoolteacher may pitch her personality against it; the athletic coach may demand its subordination to the higher loyalty to school and game, the club leader or scoutmaster may shame it into less haughty exposure in his plea for teamwork and unselfish practice, but it is a stubborn idolatry.

Self-worship enslaves the father as a being who is "always right." It produces the dominating parent

# KEEP YOURSELF FROM IDOLS 105

and "makes smotherers out of mothers" as one has so aptly said. Stubborn and arbitrary rules are hurled at children in the functions of eating, playing, washing, and so forth and give the death blow to young independence, pride and any vestige of self-reliance. When Heppel said, "Of ten wounds a child receives, nine are from its mother," he was merely warning us as to how these selfish and arrogant idolatries, especially this one of heartlessly enthroning our own opinions, can wound a child sorely.

Then there is the idol of *popularity*. This is a most prevalent god. It has enthroned itself early in life, and before marriage, on the college campus. It would almost seem that the greatest thing to the average university student today is "acceptance." The most unfortunate thing that can befall a student is to be called a "square," to be unacceptable in sorority, fraternity or dormitory life. "Conform, conform" is the cheap cry of this god, and most kneel to him easily and early. It creeps into the home—this whining cry: "But mother, everybody does it," as though that were life's highest law. Few parents counter this false god with such announcements as, "But we don't do it," or "Our morals are never at the mercy of the mob," or "This family has its own conscience." This god, who follows always the public mores, will tell us what to say, what to eat, what to drink, how to dress, where to go and what to be. Every family will need a "magnetic north" for the compass of conscience or else the needle of decision, lacking a great moral ultimate, or *summum bonum*, will vacillate crazily between public opinion and common thought until both child and adult find themselves kneeling cravenly at the feet of this god of popular public opinion. Every home must establish above itself a great moral ultimate, a magnetic north of ethical reference. Let it be God Himself.

There may also be enthroned the idol of an *idolatrous desire for things*. Against this Christ has warned us, "A man's life consisteth not in the abundance of the things which he possesseth." The world will make us think it does. Advertisements, TV and radio sponsors, billboard splashes and a thousand materialistic overtures will brainwash us into thinking that life does consist mainly of "things" and that all we have to do to live is to surround ourselves with the latest in modern gadgets and paraphernalia, discover the right filter or purchase the right car. How to curb this god of inordinate and uncontrolled desire is a problem. We must control our "wanting" as well as our acting. This craving to "get," this uncontrolled sense of "gimme" within brings about this idolatry. It will soon lead the wife to weigh her husband's worth by his ability to hang clothes on her, fill the larder with the costliest of stuffs, satisfy her buying sprees, gratify her every sense. But this god never satisfies. It leads the child to expect the extravagant present and ask the unreasonable favor and to look upon father as a human cash register whose drawer of cash easily opens at the proper manipulation. It will drive the husband and father to sacrifice all, perhaps, to achieve the desire of family and self. This god gives birth to a lust for things that is never satisfied.

Dr. Carlyle Marney recalls the short story in *The New Yorker* of the six-year-old lad who had just learned to count. He asked his mother what was the last, last, very last number he could count. The mother answered that he could count and count and count, but he could never, never, never count the last number. She turned away thinking how neatly she had slipped the concept of infinity into the mind of the little boy, but when she turned back to him, he was lying on his bed softly weeping.

It always ends there for those who worship the idol of unlimited desire. The wanting loses itself in infinity and the worshiper loses himself in frustrated despair. But how easily can this worship of things creep into the temple of the heart and of the home!

There is the god of *position*. How craftily he establishes himself! The wife may barter a great many things to attain leadership in the community. The little dwarfs of the inconsequential will keep tugging at her energy and her time. She may sacrifice anything to be president of this and that; to throw the best parties; to be the best dressed in her set; to have the best-furnished house; to master the tastiest cuisine; to win the popularity contest. It might, at the last stage, make her forget altogether that there is a difference between prominence and preëminence; between starlight and footlights; between the central and the marginal in life; between the relevant and the irrelevant. But this latter capacity fades in the strange incense burned to the god of position.

The husband too can be caught in the meshes of this idolatry—the passion to make a killing in business; to be promoted above all others; to command and even to crush, if need be; the fever to always lead; the passion to "put it over" all others. Then, subtly, time is his greatest gift to this god of position. He steals it from his children and his family to bestow it on this idol. He forgets the use of a wastebasket—the fact that there are some things to which he must say No. The click of the cash register drowns out the lad's cry for a father's companionship; the meeting of the board deluges the evening at home; he imagines that all the courtesies love demands can be cared for by the swift telegram or the present sent, as though trinkets were as needed in his home as his time! Gradually the pal becomes a provider, the man becomes a machine; the sweetheart who once was becomes the big success—and fails the home. Position is god now.

Always and ever both husband and wife, father and mother must search the niches of the house to be sure that there are no lurking idols; be quick to smell the odor of eery incense burned to these strange gods; be stern in bringing them all under the captaincy of Christ and His great increasing purpose: "Seek ye first the kingdom of God, and his righteousness; and all these things shall be added [shall be mere additions] unto you."

God must remain the great "first."

## XXII
## The Home and the Home Town

THE ENVIRONMENT IN which the home stands is of vital importance. The setting of a gem in a ring affects the impression the stone creates, adds to its apparent worth or subtracts from it. Many a painting is enhanced or handicapped by the frame surrounding it. There is strategy in a "setting."

A home can easily take on the color of its surroundings and borrow from the mores of the city in which it stands. The school, the club, the society, the church and "Main Street" make their impression upon every hearthside.

When the collegian comes "home" on vacation, there are two things in his mind: the house in which

## THE HOME AND THE HOME TOWN 109

he dwells, his "home"—and his "home town" which surrounds it. Not only will he visit his own house, he will make his call on the old campus which commandeered more of his time than any other institution, and the teachers of yesterday who had so much to do with the molding of his ideals. The corner store or ice-cream parlor that once rang with the laughter of his friends may have changed its personnel, but it has not lost its social potency. In the pew of his church old memories of God and those first glorious, troubled years will come welling back. He may stand on the sidelines of the football field or basketball floor and remember there the travail of young defeat and the thrill of youthful victory, the rigors of training and of self-denial which were a "school of life" to him. A glance at the town movie house will sum up, even unconsciously, all the ideas of life, behavior and romance that flashed before his young and alert eyes in the days when the things seen were swiftly photographed through the eyes' young lenses and put in the fixing bath of memory forever. He will recall the swimming pool or pond, the playing fields and the lanes of romance—all the things that fortified the character or tripped up the resolves of early years. The town too is "home."

Our interest and schedule as parents in the home therefore can never be confined to the hearthside alone. The home, and members of it, must reach out and shape and form and transform a city's life, for this is the atmosphere and the air that the home breathes. The home must be interested in the educational institution. My boyhood memories are vivid when I think of how our home earnestly and thoughtfully expressed its deep interest in the school and those who made it. Goethe said, "They who teach children are worthy of double the honor of those who merely bear them."

There were four children in our family—three sons and a daughter. In my early days one teacher taught all the subjects in her particular grade. Once a year my father would invite to dinner the four instructors who "wet-nursed the four young wildcats" as someone has humorously put it, and there at the table they learned the deepfelt gratitude of parental hearts. I remember my father at evening family altar, read that verse, "And they that be wise shall shine as the brightness of the firmament; and they that turn many to righteousness, as the stars for ever and ever" (Daniel 12:3). This to him was the teacher's task at its best. Then he gave a prayer of heartfelt thankfulness for the teachers who had trained and loved us, without the thrust of being kith or kin to us; he heard their problems and their joys at this festal board of thanksgiving.

I remember one of my instructors, after this expression, saying with tears in her eyes, "You know, Louis, this is the first time in twelve years of teaching that anyone thought to say thank you like this!" What easy divorcement the home and school can suffer; what a majestic team they can become!

The PTA should never be lacking in home support. After all, the teachers have children many more hours a day than parents have them. In this sense the public school can join with the church and the home in becoming the "womb of the world," where character and minds and souls are given birth and their direction determined.

In this sphere the teacher also must recognize the vast importance of the home. Too much "homework" has robbed many a home of reasonable evening companionship. School, church, community life and recreation schedules must never be permitted to rob the home of that "togetherness" that is one of its strongest gifts.

T. S. Eliot reminds us,

> What life have you if you have not life together?
> There is no life that is not in community,
> And no community not lived in praise of God.
> Even the anchorite who meditates alone,
> For whom the days and nights repeat the praise of God,
> Prays for the Church, the Body of Christ incarnate.
> And now you live dispersed on ribbon roads,
> And no man knows or cares who is his neighbour
> Unless his neighbour makes too much disturbance,
> But all dash to and fro in motor cars,
> Familiar with the roads and settled nowhere.
> Nor does the family even move about together,
> But every son would have his motor cycle
> And daughters ride away on casual pillions.

The home can become a mecca in the town for the right sort of social gatherings. It will take some planning. The basketball standards in the backyard, the Ping-pong tables set somewhere, the swimming pool, the basement playroom, the table that can be easily enlarged for friends, the freezer that cushions the shock of the sudden and uninvited young guests, just the sort of spirit of "having room" can replace the questionable pitfalls of a community's life. The hi-fi and stereo sets with ample and well-chosen record piles, the easily accessible barbecue set and easily raided icebox can tempt youth to that wholesome and merry heart that "doeth good like a medicine." There are various ways of hanging out the welcome sign in any home and the young are quick to sense it hanging there—or to decry the absence of it. Many a home has become headquarters for happy hearts and the deepest and most wholesome of friendships.

How important, too, is the "old town theater." What youths see and hear employs 95 per cent of their perceptive powers—15 per cent through hearing and 80 per cent through seeing. Any sound film then commands the bulk of their learning paraphernalia—eye and ear.

Yet how little interest and influence do parents on the average attach to what is shown in the home town's amusement places! How slow we are to praise the good and condemn the evil in these potent hours.

Laura Margaret Evans in her splendid book *Hand in Hand* has posed the problem:

We took our girls to see *The Old Man and the Sea* this evening. Our girls wept when the sharks tore into that gallant, vulnerable body of the Great Fish. Our little one said, "Oh, Daddy, I feel so sorry for the Old Man. And for the fish, too."

Then we heard a boy laugh. A boy with the half-changed voice of adolescence, and suddenly the theater was filled with short, sharp guffaws like the frenzied cries of wild coyotes. Anger grabbed me in a hot vise and I could hardly contain myself. Our modern youth —with less respect for valor and the struggle for life, with less recognition of deep emotion than wild animals. Our youth!

When it was over, we rose to take the girls home and then we noticed with surprise that the young people, junior high and high school mostly, were remaining for the second feature. And I thought, "Oh, no. They shouldn't be staying for this!" Something urged me to stay after the family left. It was Friday night and very few adults were present.

None of the youngsters left. And there was not a sound in that theater during the entire show. There was not a sound during the lewd build-up to an act of adultery. There wasn't a murmur as they soaked up the cynic's view on the utter degradation of man. No one talked through a thoroughly frank dialogue about marital impotence. And there wasn't a snicker as they listened to the account of a husband shooting another man as he climbed out of his wife's bed. Those children absorbed every word, every thought, every facial expression and each facet of that disgusting unnecessary, badly censored film.

I watched their faces as they left the theater, the bald overhead lights hitting the carefully held masks of nonchalance—but showing so pathetically the shock and dismay that lay brooding in their eyes. The light fell on the soft faces of the girls as they avoided the eyes of the boys at their sides. The hoarse young throats cleared themselves for something witty and careful to say.

I wanted to put my arms around them and say, "I'm sorry!" because anger no longer filled me. A great, sickening shame washed over me and I lowered my face from their gaze. . . .

Do their parents know what hot iron has been seared into their children's souls tonight? Have these parents even seen the movie? Probably not. Perhaps they were sitting quietly at home, watching TV, playing a harmless game of cards, having cocktails with a few friends —maybe even mentioning with a twentieth-century smile of indulgence that "the children are at the neighborhood theater seeing *The Old Man and the Sea*. Such a stirring picture. We just love our little theater. We feel so safe with the youngsters there."

What was the second feature? "Oh, just some unimportant, offbeat film. You know the type. The kids just sit and eat popcorn through those."

No, they do not just eat popcorn through those. They watch. And they listen. And they record. Like cameras, clearly and permanently. It does not matter whether it is good or bad, decent or obscene, important or offbeat. These lenses are as sensitive and precise as those which come in the German cameras their fathers pay so much money for.

An unimportant film? There is no such thing to a child. Everything is experience and truth, and he will record it as such.

How long since the average parent has gone up to the town theater manager after the showing of an obscene film and said, "I think that was rotten!"? We have simply lost our moral flashpoint in too many instances. We have lost our capacity for righteous anger. We would be angered enough should the attendant put adulterated oil into our crank case or inferior, unstrained gas into our automobile tank—we happen to love our cars! But many parents seem to take no interest at all in the sort of "stuff" that is poured into the eternal souls of their children. They would be indignant enough should poisoned goods be sold at the market but there are no "pure food laws" for the lecherous things that are sold to the minds of their children. Many of the films shown today to youth and to adults are destroying rapidly whatever moral conduct pattern America may have had, and we are reminded once again that:

> Vice is a monster of so frightful mien,
> As to be hated needs but to be seen;
> Yet seen too oft, familiar with her face,
> We first endure, then pity, then embrace.

Parents and theater managers must sit together and guard the recreational diet of any community. It can be done in spite of the "block system" of securing films behind which too many motion picture theater operators now hope to find their refuge.

But even if the public places continue to offer this scrofulous diet on occasion, has the home lost all that reasonable authority that once could say, "We will not be seeing this one"?

# XXIII

# When a Couple Prays

IT HAS BEEN well said that "the home that prays together, stays together."

There is a law in geometry and physics that when two objects are close to the same object, they of necessity have become closer to each other. This is the law of the spiritual universe as well. When husband and wife are both close to God, it is very likely that they will come close to each other. If prayer is sincere prayer, it will embrace the submission of the will of each to God, since God's will is the same as to the general purpose of our lives. Then, too, they will be teaming up on a central purpose and a common aim.

One of the greatest barriers to effective prayer will be our selfishness.

You cannot simply walk in on the President of the United States. An appointment must be made for you, either by the President, or by one of his secretaries. Naturally, they would inquire as to your business with him. Naturally God would inquire as to your business with Him, as you come into the throne room of prayer for an audience. "Thy will be done on earth as it is in heaven" (Matthew 6:10).

This must be the supreme purpose of your life and mine. If you are in a rowboat and you cast a rope out to the shoreline, what are you endeavoring to do? Pull the shoreline over to you, or pull your boat over to the shoreline? The question seems to be preposterous, but it must be asked in prayer. What are we trying to do with God? Are we trying to persuade Him to do our will, or give Him the opportunity of persuading us to do His will? We can never ask of God until, by a surrender of the will, we allow God to ask of us. This puts us in praying position, as Christians.

Many times we must pray for ourselves. Christ started His priestly prayer in this fashion: "Father, glorify thou me . . ." (John 17:5). But it was to a generous end: "That thy Son also may glorify thee" (John 17:5). He realized that He had said: "He that hath seen me hath seen the Father" (John 14:9). Therefore, if errors or mistakes touched His life, the vision of God which people saw in Him would be distorted. So this prayer for Himself was a very unselfish prayer, as it was for the glory of God.

It is quite shocking to come upon the fact now and then that many of our prayers for others are selfish prayers. A woman one day said to her minister, "I have prayed for my husband's conversion for seven years and God has not heard me. Prayer simply does not work!"

To this the minister replied, "Why do you want the salvation of your husband? Are you asking it for 'the glory of God'?"

To this she countered, "What do you mean, asking 'for the glory of God'? Is not requesting the conversion of anyone asking 'for the glory of God'?"

The minister continued, "Give me your reasons for desiring your husband's conversion, if you know them."

To this the wife replied, "Well, first of all I think that if he were a Christian he wouldn't be so mean to me. Our life would be more pleasant together."

To this the pastor replied, "Selfish reason number one. Any other?"

"Well, yes; if he were a Christian he would go to church with me and would save me the embarrassment, when I sit alone in the sanctuary, of the community's feeling that I was married to a pagan."

"Your embarrassment again. Selfish reason number two. Any other?"

"Yes, if he were a Christian I think we two could team up together and raise our children to better advantage. Then they would probably not stub their toes and we would not have to hang our heads in the community."

"So *you* would not have to hang *your* head, selfish reason number three. Now, my dear lady, this is a purely selfish prayer. You should pray in this wise and mean it, 'O God, I ask for my husband's conversion for Thy glory, and Thy glory alone. Thou dost need him in the service, and he needs Thee. Save him for Thy name's sake.'"

She prayed the prayer earnestly and honestly and came back in a week. She had received her petition. Finally, she had prayed for another unselfishly.

You may pray for yourself, too, in an unselfish manner. If you are going on a trip and you have trouble with the car—if the ignition is not working, if there is something the matter with the steering, if you have blowouts, or there is a poor functioning mechanically, you will find it quite impossible to enjoy the companionship of others in your car. You will be somewhat blinded to the beauties that are all about you, and simply will not appreciate the trip.

If you have too much trouble with yourself, with your spirit, with your disposition, you will not enjoy abiding with anybody else—in your home, in the community or in the circle of your friends. You will miss much of the beauty of life. You will just not enjoy the trip, which is made up of the years of your existence here. You must look to your own spiritual functioning. So put yourself near the top of the prayer list, but do it unselfishly.

There are types of prayer when you must "Go into your room and shut the door and pray to your Father who is *in secret;* and your Father who sees in secret will reward you" (Matthew 6:6). There are some things that we tell God, but tell no one else. There are vows which we speak to Him, at which others would smile, because of their arrogant nature. There are things we wish to say that are for the ear of God alone. This is perfectly understandable.

Then there is corporate *prayer with others.* "For where *two or three* are gathered together," there is a special blessing (see Matthew 18:20). In the first place, as we pray together our prayers become less and less selfish. The other is always taken into consideration. It is sifted through two nettings, then the small things simply pass through and out. As we pray for each other instinctively, we see ourselves in the other's words, in the other's petitions. We sense others' longings, and ambitions; their consciousness of failure and their thrill of success. If prayer is the sincere desire of the soul expressed, then our hearts are open to each other on bended knee, as they are at no other time. We can learn more of ourselves on bended knee than we can by standing on tiptoe, or by lying on the psychologist's couch. In the group others pray for us in terms of what they see lacking in us. We must dare to listen then.

There is a tremendous adhesive here. People who stay close to God find it not so difficult to stay close to each other.

Many times our prayers are not answered because we pray for *"things"* more than for people. Someone has said that the test of anyone is to put him over against his town and say, "Now, what do you see, things or faces?" This is a good question to ask before we go to our knees. Now what will I see, *things?* Do I really subtly feel that life consists in the abundance of things, or do I see *faces?* Is my chief interest in what is happening to human beings, human souls and human hearts?

The average woman becomes bored with her home, because she sees no invisible in it. She cannot see definitely how anything is being accomplished if she can't "put her finger on it"! There are some things you cannot put your fingers upon. They are intangible, valuable, eternal. A woman's housekeeping is never as important as her homemaking. What she is, is much more important than what she does. The accomplishment is in being something, more than in doing something, and here we can so miserably fail. A man is not judged merely by the size of his salary check as a provider, but also by his capacities as a partner. A woman is not to be judged by her culinary art or her ability to keep a house, but by her loving spirit and her ability to make a home. We sometimes forget this in an age of technology.

Most of our disappointments are in the realm of things. We asked for money, and we did not get it because we probably would not know what to do with it if we had it. We prayed for a large house, but we wouldn't know how to use it if we possessed it; we asked for position but what would we have done with position had we attained it? If we are not faithful in the little opportunities that God gives us to perform tasks happily, how can He trust us with larger successes and larger accomplishments? Few people become five-talent men until first they have been faithful one-talent men.

But no one ever asks sincerely for forgiveness

without receiving the peace of God. No one ever asks sincerely for power over temptation, deeply desiring it, without receiving it. No one ever asks to be Christlike, being willing to pay the price, the disciplines, without progressing in this great spiritual similarity.

The trouble is that so many of our prayers have to do with what we have instead of what we are. Adolph Schlatter, the father of the great theologian, was dying and a friend was comforting him saying, "Well, soon you will walk the golden streets, you will have the promised treasures and you will be drinking out of golden goblets." To this the aged theologian replied: "Away with that rubbish! What I want is to be in the bosom of God."

He wanted to be like God. Is that the supreme desire of our lives? Do we want His character more than cash? Would we rather be right than rich? Would we rather be purposeful than popular? Would we rather have God than gold? Prayer, you see, must be less of "give me" and more of "make me." Character is the lasting thing.

If we ask for the right things, we receive them; but so often our prayers are unanswered because we ask amiss.

It is possible in any home for a prayer for self to be quite unselfish. A father may pray for himself, for God's keeping and sustaining of himself, for the sake of a child.

> To feel his little hand in mine so clinging and so warm,
> To know he thinks me strong enough to shield him from all harm;
> To see his little childlike faith in all that I can say or do—

It sort of shames a fellow—but it makes him better too;
And I reckon I'm a better man than what I used to be
Because I have this chap at home who thinks the world of me.

I wouldn't disappoint his trust for anything on earth,
Nor let him know how little I just actually am worth.
And after all it's easier that higher road to climb
With those little hands behind me to push me all the time.
So I reckon I'm a better man than what I used to be
Because I have this chap of mine who thinks the world of me!

"O God, don't let me fall, for his sake, sustain me, keep me clean, courageous, Godlike ever." A selfless prayer for self.

A mother can feel this same unselfish petition within her soul as she calls God's blessing upon her own life for the sake of her children, knowing that at an early age they need an example more than a critic and what they see makes an indelible impression upon the young mind. Her heart may rightly cry out a prayer.

If we are but instruments in the hand of God, then let us always pray that God's hand shall be permitted to wield us as He will and thus each of us shall fashion the other and mold the other, together with our children, into His own glorious character and likeness. To pray for self with our eyes fixed beyond self —on the higher goal—is an artistry not easily attained but mighty and powerful when learned and exercised.

# XXIV

# Your Shields of Brass

THERE ARE TIMES in marriage when a brave heart parades with shields of brass instead of gold. The explanation is nestled away in Scripture in a remote part of I Kings 14.

Before this Judah knew her "golden day." David the King so blessed of Jehovah took to himself "shields of gold." Then came the glory of Solomon and he made "three hundred shields of beaten gold." Then Solomon died, and the glory of the nation perished with him.

His son Rehoboam was reigning now in his stead. But they were hard and bitter days. Shishak, mighty leader of the enemy hosts, had led them down upon Judah like wolves come down upon a fold, and "he took away all the shields of gold which Solomon had made." What should they do now? The glory had faded. Today was not as yesterday. But there was a vow of loyalty to Jehovah that had been made, there was a Kingdom yet to revere and courage to be shown and, in a sense, the banners must not touch the ground.

A crass world would never know how "the glory had fled." So instead of deserting his kingly duties and cowering in melancholy fear, Rehoboam would keep up appearances—let other hearts droop in despondency. He gave a command not to abdicate nor to surrender to the exigencies of the hour but to make shields of brass, shine them until they glittered as pure gold and parade bravely with these with unfaltering step and unsmothered courage. He "made in their stead brazen shields," and as they marched bravely from palace to temple and to palace again, no one dreamed that the glory of Judah had departed. Brave and constant souls!

In many a home the golden shields of romance have been stolen; the thievery of time or drabness or selfishness or treason or coldness have walked away with the golden shields of romance and rich newness. Marriage is no longer a parade, it is a sullen march. His job is monotonous and worn; his briefcase thrown on the divan symbolizes that the calling once so thrilling has now deteriorated into just a job. He is just a provider now, not a partner. The little gestures of once kind romance have given way to the dull mechanical recognition of the birthday and the anniversary. The romantic stroll for love's sake has given way to the brisk walk for health's sake. The golden has given way to the dull grey of life. Love, once thrilled on the mountaintop, has now drooped down to the plain. The banners of happiness and pageantry have been rolled away, surrendered now to the drudgery of commonplace living.

She too has lost that romantic touch that thrilled; love yields now—it does not leap to meet the other. The same old dishes taste insipid; compliments are more polite than passionate; the little touches that made for queenliness now give way to the conventional and the necessary. The gold and glitter have gone. Strange things and forces have drained the hearthside, and the vessels of gold are gone and the shields of gold with them. The leaden cup has replaced the golden chalice.

There are many considerations before a couple in this situation—their duty to their children, to their church, to their vow, to their community, to a kingdom. How many in such an hour have, as Rehoboam, made for themselves "shields of brass" out of the common stuff of duty, and with these have paraded so bravely that the world has never even guessed that the glory of Judah had departed? With head unbowed and duty performed they march on with a sense of royal obligation still, their stride unhindered, never at any moment truly sorry for themselves.

She goes on singing her song in the kitchen, her faithful lullaby at the cribside. With the soft cloth of feminine tenderness she polishes up the brazen mug of duty that was once a golden chalice of privilege and drinks of that cup with smiling courage, day after day. With royal, steady step she marches on through the valleys of everyday and over the hills of some days, and none would guess that for her the gold is gone and brass has taken its glorious place.

What, after all, is love? Is love the cinema idea of affection? Can this advocated "love" which is merely an amalgam of passion, sentiment, selfish satisfaction, self-seeking, the desire to be pampered, to get all and give none, to be coddled, praised and petted, be "love at its best"? True golden love is made up of duty to God and man, of unselfishness, of the desire to give more than it receives. True love "suffers long, is not easily provoked; true love endures all things, hopes all things—love never fails."

Not all joy is found in doing the easy thing, in standing by the pleasant cause. It was said of the sufferings of Christ for us, of His love for us, "who for the joy set before him endured the cross, despising the shame." Joy in a crucifixion? Yes. Not the "fun" but the "joy" of it. The deep-rooted satisfaction that accrues from doing something that is right and generous and good, even though it means drops of blood, and tears, and travail. These "cross-dodgers" in marriage never find their exaltation; because it was only after Christ's suffering that He was "exalted"—the throne of elevation came after the cross of humiliation. Nor can we reverse the order. He took an emblem of suffering, pain and death and made of it the symbol of all that is noble, joyous and glad.

Peter exclaimed, when contemplating Christ's crucifixion, "Be it far from thee, Lord" (Matthew 16:22). But He waved Peter aside, changed a brazen cross of duty into a golden cross of exaltation and now the once despised symbol is worn about the necks of gracious women, bedecks many a brave ensign, and crowns the spires of churches, who in history have learned to parade with shields of brass during days of tumult and of war.

It is perfectly possible too that as they parade with brass shields they may experience that divine alchemy that turns them into gold again. It has happened often in the empires that are called homes.

There are brave souls in the annals of God and home who have never been feted for carrying easily their shields of romantic love, but who will always be loved and admired for bearing bravely their shields of duty up over the hills and down into the valleys and then into the sun—always into the sun at the last!

# SOURCES

| Page | Line | |
|---|---|---|
| 14 | 7 | Paul Popenoe, *Love Begins at Forty*, The Institute of Family Relations, Los Angeles, California. |
| 14 | 23 | *Ibid.* |
| 25 | 22 | Author unknown. |
| 27 | 17 | Georgie Starbuck Galbraith, "The House Undivided," *The Saturday Evening Post*. |
| 28 | 3 | Author unknown. |
| 29 | 8 | James Gordon Gilkey. |
| 37 | 6 | Paul Popenoe, *The Conservation of a Family*, Williams & Wilkins Co., 1926. |
| 37 | 8 | *Ibid.* |
| 50 | 33 | Richard Chenevix Trench, "Prayer." |
| 51 | 12 | C. Milo Connick, *Build on the Rock*, Fleming H. Revell Company, 1960, page 43. |
| 54 | 16 | KJV. |
| 55 | 1 | KJV. |
| 55 | 6 | KJV. |
| 55 | 18 | From *The Man and Book Nobody Knows* by Bruce Barton, copyright 1924, 1956, used by special permission of The Bobbs-Merrill Company, Inc., the publishers. |
| 62 | 1 | C. Milo Connick, op. cit., page 138. |
| 62 | 11 | *Ibid.*, page 139. |
| 63 | 3 | KJV. |
| 63 | 18 | *Ibid.* |
| 65 | 28 | KJV. |
| 68 | 33 | KJV. |
| 71 | 5 | Helmuth Thielicke, *The Waiting Father*, Harper & Brothers, 1959, copyright by John Doberstein. |

| Page | Line | |
|---|---|---|
| 74 | 8 | KJV. |
| 76 | 27 | KJV. |
| 77 | 14 | Amber Blanco White, "Worry in Women." |
| 77 | 23 | KJV. |
| 79 | 27 | KJV. |
| 80 | 24 | KJV. |
| 81 | 26 | Theodore Monod, "None of Self and All of Thee." |
| 82 | 28 | KJV. |
| 82 | 35 | KJV. |
| 84 | 29 | Margaret E. Sangster, "Our Own." |
| 85 | 25 | A paraphrase of Mark 10:8. |
| 87 | 3 | Mazie V. Caruthers, "Prayer of Any Husband," from *Masterpieces of Religious Verse*. Reprinted by permission Harper & Brothers. |
| 87 | 21 | KJV. |
| 88 | 15 | KJV. |
| 88 | 18 | KJV. |
| 91 | 1 | Author of first stanza unknown; second verse by Dr. Evans |
| 92 | 5 | Alfred Tennyson, "Locksley Hall." |
| 93 | 23 | Henry Wadsworth Longfellow, "The Song of Hiawatha." |
| 96 | 29 | C. Milo Connick, op. cit., pages 116, 117. |
| 97 | 33 | John Kendricks Bangs, "On File," *The World's Best-loved Poems*, Thomas Gilchrist Lawson, comp., Harper & Brothers, 1927. |
| 108 | 11 | KJV. |
| 111 | 5 | T. S. Eliot, "Choruses From 'The Rock.'" |
| 112 | 13 | Laura Margaret Evans, *Hand in Hand*, Fleming H. Revell Company, 1960, page 45ff. |
| 114 | 17 | Alexander Pope, "Essay on Man." |
| 115 | 21 | KJV. |
| 116 | 8 | KJV. |
| 116 | 11 | KJV. |
| 120 | 30 | Author unknown. |
| 125 | 9 | KJV. |

# MORE CHALLENGING READING FROM YOUR FAVORITE AUTHORS
## Complete and Unabridged

**GOD'S PSYCHIATRY by Charles L. Allen** 95¢
An actual working manual which can change your life in just seven days. From Biblical lessons come ways to banish fear, acquire confidence, and face life with new enthusiasm and peace of mind.

**THE BURDEN IS LIGHT! by Eugenia Price** 75¢
The amazing autobiography of a successful, sophisticated writer whose empty personal life was transformed when she took the Word of God literally!

**A MAN CALLED PETER by Catherine Marshall** 1.25
The glowing story of the acclaimed minister and Senate chaplain whose messages touched the heartstrings of the whole world.

**PEACE WITH GOD by Billy Graham** 95¢
Written by one of the century's most influential religious figures, here is inspiration and comfort for the man in the street.

**ANGEL UNAWARE by Dale Evans Rogers** 75¢
The poignant story of the birth, and death, of Roy and Dale Rogers' own little girl. A lasting victory over great sorrow.

**THROUGH GATES OF SPLENDOR by Elisabeth Elliot** 95¢
An on-the-scene account of the martyrdom of five American missionaries in the steaming jungles of Ecuador, an epic of unmatched courage and faith.

**THE LITTLE PEOPLE by David Wilkerson** 95¢
Conceived in hate, born without love, robbed of their childhood—these are the children of addicts and prostitutes, muggers and alcoholics. Here is their story, who they are, how they exist, and what happens to them.

# ORDER FROM YOUR BOOKSTORE

*If your bookstore does not stock these books, order from*

**SPIRE BOOKS**
**Box 150, Old Tappan, New Jersey 07675**
Please send me the books indicated. Enclosed is my payment plus 15¢ mailing charge on first book ordered, 10¢ each additional book.

Name_____

Address_____

City_____ State _____ Zip_____

_____ Amount enclosed __Cash __Check __Money order (No c.o.d.'s)